Central Asian Art

Page layout: Julien Depaulis

ISBN : 1 90431 041 9

Printed in Singapore

Central Asian Art

Summary

Title page: Tilakari madrasah in Samarkand.

BRIEF GLANCE
AT HISTORY

Central Asia, ancient territory where nature offers contrasts different from any other country in the world, traditionally regroups four republics of the community of Independent States: Kirghizstan, Tadjikistan, Turkmenistan and Uzbekistan, extending from the Caspian Sea to the Chinese border. Broad deserts and flourishing orchards and vineyards, snow-covered mountains and green valleys, old abandoned cities, traditional villages and modern towns proud of their past - often several thousand years old, and with famous monuments - may be found here. Centre of successive civilisations and multiple cultures, this vast area claims an exceptional architectural, artistic and handicraft heritage.

Ever since the Bronze Age and the beginning of the Iron Age, Central Asia has rivalled with classical Eastern Asia (which extended from Mesopotamia to India) in the abilities and skills of its peoples. In the 6th century B.C. it was largely conquered by the powerful Achaemenian Dynasty and in the 4th century B.C. by Alexander the Great's army which gave it considerable artistic impetus. The period between the 3rd century B.C. and the 3rd century A.D. marked the area with the appearance of powerful Kingdoms : the Parthians of the Arsacian dynasty (south of Turkmenistan, in Persia and in part of Mesopotamia), the Greco-Bactrians, the Kushans (which included Bactria and the territory beyond Amu-Daria as far as the Indus and the Ganges) the Kangas (that united the Kharezm, the Sogdian and the northern territories) whose social and cultural development founded a cultural impulse entirely new throughout the territory they controlled.

If the development of the arts in Central Asia was closely linked with their neighbours, this period was nevertheless marked by a conjunction of influences, Hellenistic, Indo-Buddhist and South Persian, whereas in the North-East, the central territories, the Sakas and the Scythians, left the imprint of their own traditions. But the local artists didn't satisfy themselves with copying shapes and designs alien to them, but modified, according to their sensibility, the forms and the content of foreign cultures. They worked with their own ancestral techniques and according to their aesthetic sense and ideology, thus giving birth to a new art profoundly original at the threshold of the 4th century B.C.

Tilakari madrasah in Samarkand.

The fall of the ancient empires of Central Asia and the invasions of the 4th and 5th century by wandering tribes from the North predetermined the establishment of a new social order, an intensive feudal system and the constitution of a great number of semi-independent principalities. It was a period of domination by rich landowners who lived in innumerable fortresses scattered in the plains and in the mountains. One of the most remarkable characteristics of this renewed social system was the formation of a particular type of medieval culture in the towns, then few in number, and the development of many crafts in different artistic areas.

The political dismemberment encouraged the conquest of the region by the Arabs and its submission to the Caliphate Power from the 7th century. It was at this time that all the countries between the Amu-Daria and the Semirechiye (the Seven Rivers' country) was named Mavera-un-nahr. The south of the present Turkmenistan became a part of Khorasan's province and only Kharezm kept its former name.

Previous Page: Walls of Boukhara's old citadel.

The mausoleum of the Tilakari madrasah in Samarkand.

Ruins of the village of Toprak Kala in Uzbekistan.

Islam Khodja minaret in Khiva.

Mohammed Rakhim-Khan madrasah
in Khiva.

A part of the patrimony, including mural paintings, sculptures and representative figures opposed to the Arab laws about ornament, was destroyed during that period, but at the same time, many aspects of artistic life were influenced by Muslim culture.

During the 10th and 12th century, art again met with many sudden changes. Ancient traditions were abandoned, the development of monumental paintings and sculptures ceased and the ornamental, decorative style common to all Islamic countries in architecture and the applied arts became the main source of creation. On political grounds, the local noblemen, even when they were nominally subjects of the Caliphate, began to conduct their States with total independence from the 9th and 10th century.

At last, at the beginning of the 11th century, following the numerous Turkomen invasions, the Turkomen dynasties established themselves in this region. This period favoured the development of urban culture and the growth of towns, among which Merv - today abandoned - Samarkand, Khiva and Bukhara remained representative of the essential spirit.

Around 1150 the architecture of Central Asia was monochrome, but in the middle of the 12th century blue brick began to be used and considerable progress was made in the art of building and in decorative ornamentation. But the Turco-Mongol invasions at the beginning of the following century put a stop to all artistic development for almost a hundred years.

It was only at the end of a slow revival that a renewal began to appear in the 15th century, under the reign of Tamerlan and the Timurids, today considered the most sumptuous of the artistic patrimony of Central Asia. The edifices from that time are characterized by their decorative aspects and the richness of colour of the glazed ornaments.

The palette of the ceramic surfaces became more and more varied, with a predominance for turquoise blue. Under Timur, in the 1470's, Samarkand experienced a great development in architecture, which is a testimony to the power of the Governor.

The edifices of this time are remarkable for their monumental conception intended to strike people's eyes and hearts. The variety of decorative techniques, glazed bricks, majolica tiles, sculptured baked clay are proof of a great artistic mastery. With similar ideas concerning the edifices meant for worship, buildings for different purposes were also erected for the comfort of the population: takis and tims or copula galleries for trading caravanserais; public baths, bridges and sardobas or water-cisterns. The latter were of more modest proportions and surfaces.

The mausoleum Gur i-Emir in Samarkand.

Ourganch-the-Old. The mausoleum of Toura Bek Khatoun. Interior ceiling, not restored.

These traditions continued for two centuries, under the Uzbeks of the Cheibanid and the Ashtarkhanid dynasties. But the weakening of the economic and politic links outside Central Asia, victim of feudal internal wars, led to a great social crisis at the end of the 18th century.

The effect was deeply felt on cultural activities in every region except in khanate of Khiva where the economic and politic conditions remained favourable. It was only during the following century under the Emirate of Bukhara, the khanates of Khiva and of Kokand that culture knew its new Golden Age. It was at the same time, as these two khanates were integrated to the Russian Empire, that the territories of Central Asia took the names of Turkestan and Transcaspian Province.

Following Central Asia's historic destiny, its creative activities knew another sumptuous rise which was followed by a decline.

One of the mythical tents reconstructed for the 1000th birthday of Manas, Kirghiz national hero.

However, despite the period, it was through architecture, craftsmanship and illuminated design of manuscripts that the Uzbek, Turkman, Tadjin and Khirgiz artists gave the best of themselves. After the October Revolution, Central Asia was integrated into the autonomous Soviet Socialist Republic of Turkestan, that later on, conforming to the principle of national Leninist politics, was divided into four Independent Soviet Republics, until the dismemberment of the empires and their integration in the CEI.

New forms of art appeared at this time, such as easel painting, graphic arts and theatre decoration as well as monumental paintings and sculpture, abandoned years and years before, now enjoying an encouraging renewal. A powerful impulse was also given to the development of traditional applied arts, where modernity combined with the heritage of a faraway past, which was always present.

A summer encampement on the way from Kyzyl Bel to Kirghizstan.

Macoki-Attari mosque in Bukhara.

Khiva, Kunia-Ark
fortress, portal.
19th century.

21

Chir-Dor madrasah in Samarkand.
Architect Abdoul Jabbar. 1619-1631.

23

ARCHITECTURE

The architectural heritage of Central Asia offers a great diversity. The oldest period is characterized by the vestiges of mighty castles, houses, workshops, palaces, temples decorated with mural paintings and sculptures. Of these edifices nothing remains nowadays but pieces of walls, bases, fragments of columns or capitals on which can be seen elements of old western or Hellenistic architecture. During the Middle Ages (6th-8th century) particular attention was given to the building of edifices dedicated to worship, palaces, fortresses. The decoration of palaces and houses with paintings and sculptures was ample and so was sculpture on wood or on stucco, primary elements in architectural ornamentation that was to blossom during the following centuries. The medieval castles constituted one of the most characteristic forms of architecture in Central Asia. Their forms were simple and severe: over a vast terrace of beaten earth, bind walls were raised and sometimes decorated with engaged columns.

Triumph of Islam

Most of the monuments preserved until today, however, have come from a more recent period that coincides with the triumph of Islam. Ever since this epoch we have seen an increase in the construction of secular buildings (private houses, palaces, caravanserais, covered markets) as well as edifices dedicated to the cult (mosques, minarets, madrasahs, hospices for the dervishes) and some that have an intermediary place between civil and religious architecture (mausoleums). This general construction gave the medieval towns of Central Asia their peculiar aspect that we also find in Bukhara, Samarkand, Khiva, where the mosques' cupolas, the rectangular portals, the vertical lines and minarets rise above the lower part of the town, with low-roofed houses and winding alleys. In the monumental architecture, kiln bricks began to be used: not only were they going to assure longer life to the construction, but they were going to play an important part as decorative material. The oldest brick monument is the Ismail Samanid mausoleum in Bukhara, built between the 9th and 10th century. Its composition is extremely simple: a cube covered by a semi-spherical dome adorned with little corner cupolas. All the side façades are identical. The base, the central arches, the corner columns and the arcade are striking. The same clearness is to be found in the inner arrangement: simple lines of the walls with arches above, in an octagonal tambour supporting the central dome. Inside and outside the mausoleum is decorated with an ornamental masonry of bricks. The decoration resulting from the varied disposition of fine square bricks, of disks and rosettes give importance to the principal architectural forms.

Taki-Zargaron, domes of the covered market. 15th – 16th century.

Minature from the 15th century depicting the construction of a mosque in Samarkand.

Bukhara, Bekha-ad-Dim complex, ceiling in the summer mosque. 16th century.

Following page: Bukhara, Khamata Fayzabad, almshouse. 16th century.

Bukhara, madrasah Mîr-e 'Arab, main iwân vault.

The art of decoration

The mausoleum of Arab-Ata at Tim (Uzbekistan), dated 977, is the first type of funerary monument with portal and cupola. Its facade is emphasized by a monumental portal topped by a gracious blind arch. The principal ornamentation - brick masonry or sculpted stucco - is concentrated on the portal. Geometrical ornaments (ghirikh) begin to appear as well as the first epigraphic decorations, like the one on the façade. Central Asian people are particularly fond of ornaments. Geometrical and vegetal designs, abstract or epigraphic, cover practically everything - from the portals of the palaces to snuff-boxes. During the 10th and the 12th century, geometrical ornaments acquired a theoretical foundation, due to an astonishing impetus given in the East by mathematics and particularly by applied geometry. From the time

Central Asia was drawn into the Muslim orbite, epigraphic ornament acquired an entirely new character. The inscriptions in Arabic - of religious moral inspiration - had a definite goal. Their aesthetic effect contributed to the expansion of the Islamic dogma. But in many cases (as in the mausoleum of Arab-Ata), these inscriptions also contain historical information (dates - names - sometimes the names of the builders). The calligraphers must have written the texts with great exactitude and care for the beauty of the Arabic writing, proportions, harmony and rhythm. During the 10th century the architectural decoration adopted a severe style, with Kufic lettering, and during the 11th and 12th century a more pleasant and complex lettering began to appear as well as other calligraphy with more fluide lines, the naskhi.

Abd-al-Aziz Khan madrasah, vault.
17th century.

Khiva, Palhavan-Mahmud mausoleum.
19th century.

Samarkand, Tilakari madrasah.
17th century.

During this period local architectural schools appeared and proved their originality even in the elaboration of traditional artistic themes. The variations in the handling of volumes and the diversity of decorative solutions gave to each edifice an aspect of its own.

It suffices to compare the groups of karakhan mausoleums of the 11th and 12th century at Uzgen, the Sandjar mausoleum at Merv (1140), the Fakhr-ad-Dine-Razi mausoleum at Kunia-Urgench (12th century), the coupled mausoleums Hodja-Machad at Saëd (12th century), to feel all the artistic richness of the buildings of that period.

Predominance of religious art

Mausoleums and mosques are present in all Muslim towns. The great mosques are particularly sumptuous. They are distinguished by their important dimensions, their portals, their large courtyards surrounded by a gallery having a portico with columns, the iwan, at its central point. The minaret stands near the outer angle. The architectural decoration of the monuments of the 11th and 12th century is of an astonishing variety. Different forms of bricks, sculptures on wood, stucco, baked clay are used as ornament. Carved in deep relief on two or three faces, the baked clay is a newly acquired technique of the builders of Central Asia in the architectural field.

Khiva, Mohammed Rakhim-Khan madrasah. 19th century.

Khiva, Itchan-Kala, city walls.

Ramparts on Khiva's dry earth.

Islam Khodja minaret in Khiva.

Khiva, Itchan-Kala street.

Samarkand, mosque mihrab, Chakhi-
Zinde necropolis. 15th century.

'Saodat' Tchaikhana, interior. 1984.

Some remarkable examples are to be seen in the sculpture of the mausoleums of Uzgen, Kunia-Urgench and Saëd.

The ornament results from the bricks' disposition, sculptured bricks and potter's clay are mingled in their aspect and colouring with construction materials so that only their decorative design appears.

Announcing polychromy that would triumph in the following centuries, appeared bricks and tiles enamelled in blue for the surfaces of the domes or appliqued ornaments inserted into the ornamental design of the walls. Geometrical motifs dominated.

The diversity and complexity are such that it is difficult to decipher structure.

The golden age of the builders

After the Mongol invasion and its train of destruction, construction reappeared in Central Asia. The 14th century saw the construction of the mausoleum of Mohammed Baschscha, the mausoleum Gumbaz Manas and the Kubba of the Sufi dynasty, called the Turabek-Khanum mausoleum. The most important masterpieces of monumental architecture were erected during the second third of the 14th century and the first third of the 15th century under the reign of Timur (Tamerlan) who forcibly used the best builders of his immense empire, and under the reign of his grandson Ulug-Beg who erected majestic mosques and madrasahs, a great number of mausoleums, palaces, caravanserais and covered markets, in Samarkand as well as in Bukhara.

Tashkent, Museum of Applied Arts in Uzbekistan, interior. 20th century.

Dusanbe, 'Saodat' Tchaikhana, ceiling decoration. 1984.

37

They are famous for the harmony of their forms, the boldness of their architecture and the richness of their ornaments. Today one can also admire the imposing ruins of the palace Ak-Sarai at Chakhri-Siabz, entirely covered with polychrome alabaster mosaics, and the great Mosque of Tamerlan at Samarkand.

This mosque, called Bibi-Khanum (one of Tamerlan's wives who inspired many legends) was to outshine all the mosques of the Islamic world, according to the architect who planned it. Particular attention was attached to mausoleums. Some were majestic, such as the tomb of the Timurid called Gur i-Emir at Samarkand, which is one of the gems of Islamic Art. Others are smaller and of gracious forms, such as the numerous mausoleums of the Chakhi-Zinde necropolis. One of the most striking works by the architect of the Timurid is the madrasah of Ulug-Beg at Samarkand, with a façade emphasized by a high portal and four minarets at the angles. All the walls are covered in azure, turquoise and gold mosaics. The edifices of the 14th and 15th century are dominated by polychrome decoration in glazed bricks, baked clay. The same process is used for the inside decorations and sometimes the polychrome paintings are enriched with gold. Ornamental sculpture on wood or stone also became more important at this epoch.

There were also new tendencies in the ornamentation; plant motifs predominate rather than geometrical ones. They were composed of coloured bricks on vast portions of walls or around the minaret towers. The new style also affected the ornamental inscriptions. Sentences with geometrical designs are inscribed on the outside surface of the edifices. Friezes and borders are also used with inscriptions in ligatural lettering (souls). These architectural ensembles are a remarkable accomplishment of this epoch.

Many of them are striking because of the grandiose character of their forms, the precise projection of architectural volumes such as the Registan at Samarkand, largely rebuilt in the 17th century. Others, such as Chakki-Zinde are picturesque compositions with groups of little mausoleums and mosques erected in remembrance of a venerated person, along a narrow lane on a hillside in place of the old Aphrasiab. This ensemble, from the spectator's point of view, is seen as a new combination of volumes sometimes unexpected. The picturesque impression is emphasized by the richness of the polychrome ornamentation of the surface.

Previous Page: Bukhara, Bolo-Khaouz mosque. 16th century.

Ourganch-the-Old, façade of the mausoleum of Toura Bek Khatoun.

Bukhara, Kaliar mosque, entrance portal. 16th century.

The monumental architecture of Central Asia of the 16th and 17th century brought very few changes to the outside aspects of the edifices. But the interior architecture, on the contrary, improved with the elaboration of a new type of vault.

The interior decoration of the edifices in Bukhara is particularly rich. The cupolas seem separated from the walls by bay windows giving light or by stalactite corbelling that seems to float on a geometrical trellis-work complex that decorated the trompes.

The earth tiles that adorn the surface, even if they are not of the same quality and have repetitive decorative designs, continued to play an important role in the architectural decoration. But, as in the past, the artistic trades linked to architecture are of high quality.

The ceilings, doors, columns, panels and tombstones demonstrate high artistic form, particularly in the wood and stone sculptures. Still faithful in many points of the process of composition to the previous epochs, architects find new solutions for urban construction. Sometimes two monumental edifices were raised face to face such as the Kalian mosque and the Arab-Ata madrasah, the Madorikhan and Abduliakan madrasahs, the Ulug-Beg and Abd-al-Aziz-Khan madrasahs at Bukhara.

Sometimes the space is closed by three different edifices as is the case for the Registan of Samarkand bordered on three of its sides by madrasahs or the ensemble Liabi-Khauz at Bukhara around a square with a basin in the middle. The memorial ensembles usually have an informal disposition, like Tchor-Bakr at Bukhara and Cheikh-Khantaur at Tashkent.

Bukhara, Nadir-Divan-Beghi madrasah, main façade. 16th century.

The construction of monumental edifices was resumed in Central Asia at the end of the 18th century and at the beginning of the 19th century after a hundred years of cultural stagnation. Khiva, the old capital of the khanate of Khiva that appeared and was developed mainly in the 9th and 10th century, is astonishing in this respect.

The wall that encloses the centre of the town (Itchan-Kala) has kept its former appearance, with its majestic madrasahs, its mosques and their minarets, its palaces and covered markets (bazars) with houses in-between with blind façades huddled together, with little courtyard and iwans with slender columns.

Following the narrow alleys, new combinations of architectural volumes can be discovered with their wall surfaces, the vertical lines of the minarets topped with cupolas.

In the decoration of the most sumptuous edifices of Khiva, small tiles of blue and white majolica enhanced with black and white vegetal patterns, largely prevailed. Incidentally in the architectural forms, the palace decorations and the edifices dedicated to the cult, numerous motifs were borrowed from popular architecture (courtyards and iwans with columns) and from the applied arts (columns and carved doors, painted walls and ceilings, abstract and floral ornaments prevailed).

Bukhara, Kalian minaret.
12th century.

Pahlavan Mahmud complex,
19-20th century.

Bukhara, Magoki-Attari mosque.
12-16th century.

Samarkand, Gur i-Emir mausoleum,
interior. 15th century.

Samarkand, Gur i-Emir mausoleum,
interior. 15th century.

Samarkand, Gur i-Emir mausoleum,
tomb of Tamerlan and the Timurides.
15th century.

Tradition and modernity

The cultural heritage of Central Asia in the 19th century and at the beginning of the 20th century kept what the centuries and millenia of its earlier history has been able to transmit to us: examples of great constructions. The diversity of architectural types and decorative techniques are present in the habitations of the upper middle class, in the mosques of the villages and in the country. They differ due to regional climatic conditions rather than to old architectural traditions. The important towns of Central Asia had regional decorative schools which were formed on the basis of local tradesmen's corporations. In spite of similarities in decorative composition principles, the artistic techniques of these centres were different, in the wood carving as well as in the details of ornaments and colours. Thanks to an exuberant wealth, sculpted columns, carved doors, "claustras" and perforated stucco panels, painted walls and ceilings, gave great beauty to the insides of the houses and mosques.

From the establishment of the Soviet power a vast program of urbanisation was set up in Central Asia. One of the tendencies of modern architecture drew upon the national heritage. In the first place, the modern architecture which borrowed traditional planning from medieval architecture took into account the natural conditions particular to each region (aeration systems, principles of orientation, antiseismic measures). Many elements common to the old architecture were introduced with great success in the planning of the edifices, such as the ogival arches, the vaulted iwans or the stalactites with monumental forms which may protect from the sun. Modern urban architecture takes its inspiration mainly form traditional decoration. An original inspiration in the technique of glazed earthenware tiles was realized in 1927 on the pedestal of the Lenin monument at Achkhabad, where the majolica shapes imitate the motifs and colouring of a Turkman carpet.

Samarkand, Gur i-Emir mausoleum.
15th century.

Samarkand, Gur i-Emir mausoleum, portal. 15th century.

Tomb of Koussam-Ibn Abbasiecle. 14th century.

Anonymous mausoleum in Chakhi-Zinde. 14th century.

Samarkand, Amir-Zade mausoleum. 14th century.

Kunia-Urgench, Sufi mausoleum,
cupola. 14th century.

Samarkand, Ziaratkhana, place for
celebration of the Office of the Dead,
cupola detail.

Samarkand, Hahja-Akhmad
mausoleum. 14th century.

Samarkand, Chakhi-Zinde necropolis.
14th – 15th century.

Merv, Kiz-Kala. 6-8th century.
Background, Sandjar
mausoleum.

Saed, Hodja-Machad mausoleum. 9th
– 12th century.

Following page:
Kunia-Urgench, Fakhr-ad-Dine-Razi
mausoleum. 12th century.

Bukhara, mausoleum of the
Samanides, 9th – 10th century.

The perforated panels of geometrical motifs adorned the Uzbek and Tadjik pavilions at the National Agricultural Exposition of Moscow in 1937.

They were executed by popular artists. The great Navoï Theatre, built in Tashkent during the years 1940-1947, is a real laboratory of artistic co-operation between Soviet architects and the best craftsmen of Uzbek applied arts.

During the last decade, traditional architecture, ornamental sculpture and monuments have often been used by popular Uzbek, Tadjiks and Turkmen artists (the artists of Kirghizstan preferring national motifs worked in felt or leather appliqué) for the decoration of public establishments, museums, cultural palaces, rural clubs and metropolitan stations.

60

SCULPTURE

According to biblical legend, God shaped the first man from the dust of the ground. This myth explains the conception of the generation of this distant epoch, clay being the essential material used for modelling. In Central Asia, nature has been generous and clay that can be used by man was plentiful everywhere. This is why in this area the sculptures were mainly in clay rather than in wood, plaster or stone.

Statuary

Hellenism was a powerful inspiration in the development of plastic art in Central Asia. The importation of Greek statues or their execution locally by sculptors of the Hellenistic school have been corroborated by archaeological discoveries.

Ossuary. 6th – 7th century.
Art History Institute. Tashkent.

Foot of sacrifical table. 3rd – 5th century A.D. Issyk-Kul region.

Hellenistic contributions

Hellenistic art excerts its influence directly in Bactria and in the eastern regions of the Parthian realm. For instance, the Head of Heracles from the Khaltchayan palace is remarkable for the expression of the face which bears the dramatic imprint of inner sufferings, a dominating accomplishment of Hellenistic sculpture. But this aesthetic conception would soon blend into a purely Asiatic understanding of the tasks and forms of art. The representations of Heracles and Athena in the Khaltchayan palace already offer serious modifications to the local culture: Athena's face is far from having the majesty of Zeus' daughter. Only the form of her helmet makes her recognizable.

At the beginning of our era several important centres of culture already existed. At Khaltchayan, reliefs were mainly realised in painted clay. They were among the mural compositions with numerous figures where the heads of the characters were worked in high relief and even in round bosse. The themes of sculptural cycles essentially celebrate the ruling dynasty of the monarchs at the beginning of the Khushan Empire. There were scenes of solemn ceremonies and heroic exploits: the royal couple on their thrones, their family and noblemen, a victorious battle. On the frieze, children are represented wearing heavy garlands on their shoulders. In the garland's curves are inserted small half-figures of disguised people, satyrs, actors, young girls with musical instruments. All are part of a feast, a theatrical representation, or a remembrance of the Dionysiac games. This kind of frieze came from the eastern region of the Parthian kingdom as far as the Kharezm Province. At Staraia-Nissa and Toprak-Kala matrices in baked or unbaked clay have been discovered; the first are moulds of an actor's mask, his mouth open, the other a simple face with a flat nose, pointed ears and satyr's horns.

Realistic and expressive, the sculptures of Khaltchayan do not define the authenticity of the portrait but only show an ethnic type and the model's age and temperament.

Head of Kushan prince.
1st century. Art History Institute.
Tashkent.

Governor seated on his throne. Late
1st century B.C.- early 1st century.
Fragments.
Art History Institute. Tashkent.

Statue of dignitary. 1st century.
Art History Institute. Tashkent.

Buddhist influence

During the first centuries of our era, Bactrian sculpture received a strong Buddhist influence from India. The statues and reliefs at Airtam and Stary-Termez follow the Buddhist canons, but at the same time keep the stamp of the local school of sculpture.

The high-relief in white stone of the Fayaz-tépé monastery at Termez, represents Buddha seated in the shade of a tree surrounded by monks who look at him with a very canonical humility. The buildings of the Airtam monastery are also decorated with sculptures in white stone. Excavations brought to light fragments of a great statue of Buddha and more recently a monumental block with an inscription in Bactrian-Khushan where Khuvichka, king of the Kushan, Shodia, the founder of the monastery and the master Mikhrzad, probably a sculptor are mentioned. The sculptures over the inscription are supposed to represent Shodia and his wife (the figures are only half preserved). The legs are naked. The woman wears an ample garment. Her legs are crossed, bracelets adorn her ankles, characteristic details of Hindu art. Using real people as models of minor gods of Buddhist mythology, Bactrian sculptors were less restricted by the canons and were freer in their creations. Executed with the technique of sculpture in clay or plaster, the inhabitants of the sky (deva) of Dalverzine-tepe, with their young and tender faces and curly hair divulge the models of Praxitele's school. The delicate sculpture, creating a rich clair-obscure effect, the slight smile, the pensive gaze, all this gives a great spirituality to the faces. Representing the laity, the sculptors of Dalverzine-tépé try to create not realistic but idealised portraits. Although the individual lines of the face are preserved, signs of age, character or emotional state are absent. The social position of each character on the hierarchic scale is expressed by its size. The members of the dynasty are larger than life, their wives half their size, the noblemen even smaller.

Buddha and monks. 2nd century.
Museum of the History of the Peoples
of Uzbekistan. Tashkent.

Kharezm sculptures

The process gradually leading to abstraction in representations appears in the Kharezm sculptures. The man's head of Giaour-Kala (1st and 2nd century) with the face's plasticity carefully elaborated is full of a nervous tension that seems to reflect the mood of the model. The sculptures of Kharezm at Toprak-kala (2nd and 3rd century) where the central theme is the celebration of the dynasty in power, are differently perceived.

An example is the plaster fragment of a great king's head crowned by a conical royal toque. The face marked by years with eyes wide open and knitted brows is a bit stylized and conventional.

In spite of the diversity of their aspects, the figures of military chiefs, sovereigns and gods were distinguished by the absolute impassibility of their faces and their distant giving them a certain transcendency.

Sogdian sculptures

Sogdian sculptures in Central Asia were already noted in the 3rd century and early 4th century by their styles. In the sanctuary of the old town of Er-Kurgan, near Karchi, fragments of clay statues have been discovered dating from this time. The fragment of a head, summarily sculpted and enhanced by painting posseses something archaic that reflects the style of the ancient east. Two men's heads found at the same place on a great flagstone of clay show the Sogdian ethnic type: face with wide eyebrows and almond eyes, flat nose, long twisted moustache and pointed beard. They probably represent noblemen, as is testified by their crowns bordered with a strand of pearls. The faces' plasticity is expressive.

Ossuary in the form of a seated person. 1st - 2nd century.
Museum of the History of the Peoples of Uzbekistan. Tashkent.

Bactrian sculptures

Plastic art in Central Asia presents notable changes in the 3rd and early 4th century. Even though the acquired knowledge of the preceding epochs are preserved, new artistic norms appear. This can be seen distinctly in the sculptures discovered in the sun-driedbrick houses large enough to include several reception rooms which contain many luxurious decorative objets. The clay statues are painted. The heads are in round bosse and high relief. The compositions include the royal couple, and a group of women (with two dancers and two servants). Compared with Bactrian statues of high dignitaries of the preceding epochs, those of Kuev-Kurgan present another ethnic type. Furthermore, these people wear different garments, in particular the headgear of the king, with two wings, as in Central Asia during the 4th century. The heavy eyelids half shut the almond eyes, letting out a piercing gaze which gave the face a particular expression.

The early Middle Ages

The period of the early Middle Ages introduces a great number of new social ideas in the East to which the masters of the artistic culture reacted with great attention. During the 6th and 8th century, painting and the decorative arts blended with architecture and entered into decoration, not only in cultural edifices but also in civil construction: palaces, castles and private houses of rich people, bazars and caravanserai.

Buddhist art

Monumental art always maintains its place in Buddhist communities. The Buddhist constructions at Ak-Bechim, the Krasnoretchenski citadel at Kuva, Adjina-tépé and Kalai-Karfirnigan are decorated with painted clay sculptures portraying the traditional iconography of the Buddhas, the Bodhisattvas, monks, orants and other deities.

The Buddha's statues, representations particularly revered, had considerable dimensions. In this way the zealous defenders of Buddhism wanted to increase the authority of their religion that was losing its prestige in Central Asia and among its adepts. The representation of Buddha followed the canon, elaborated and fixed during the first centuries of our era according to three conceptions: sitting Buddha in a meditative attitude, having acquired the Truth; Standing Buddha, bearer and preacher of this Truth; Buddha lying on his right side in a position of supreme serenity and waiting for nirvana.

Kharezmian goddess. 2nd -1st century B.C. Ethnographical Institute of the Academy of Sciences. Moscow.

Lion's head. 6th century. Fine Arts Museum of the Uzbekistan Republic. Tashkent.

73

Head of a Warrior. 2nd – 3rd century.
Toprak-Kala. The Hermitage.
St Petersburg.

Buddha is shown with a serene inward-looking expression, slightly smiling, hair arranged in a series of artistically-placed spiral curls, contrasting with the smooth face and the ancient expression of profound meditation and great wisdom that were given to him in the previous epochs.

The same contrasts are to be seen in the Bodhisattva's faces. Their silhouettes remain lithe and well built but the shape of the body is only outlined, while necklaces and pleats of garments tightened with a belt are elaborated in detail. Secular faces are presented in a different manner. They are more realistic in spite of their idealized lines, probably executed from nature such as, for instance, women's heads from Adjina-tépé: round, naive faces with a little smile and a tender gaze. The faces of Kashyapa, fire worshipper monk and one of the bodhisattva are marked by age and meditation.

The Buddhist sculpture of this period distinguishes itself by increased interest in demonic creatures inspiring terror. They are mainly depicted by threatening demi-gods, bellicose defenders of Buddhism. Among the enormous heads of the Kuva sanctuary, a Mandjucha with a furious glance, a flat nose and a twisted mouth with hooked teeth can be seen, or the *dhachite* with a cruel woman's face wearing a crown adorned with skulls.

Mythological art

On the carved wood reliefs of Pendjikent and Kalai-Kakhkakh, mythological characters are represented, among which a winged lion, a goddess riding a lion, a rider overwhelming a wild animal.

The composition of multiple figures adorning a door tympanum from the Kalai-Kakhkakh palace is particularly expressive. There is a fantastic creature resembling a man, flanked by two riders as well as the double figure of a *peri* with long braids sitting on a two-headed bird. The subject of the panels refer to the legend of Zahak.

The popular revolt directed by the blacksmith Kave and the army of the valorous Feridun destroyed Zahak and his allies. In this fight, the rebels were helped by a higher force, coming from the sky in the form of a *peri* with long braided hair.

Inspired by this epic tale, the sculptor introduced into it the chivalrous spirit of Central Asia. Gallant warriors on their galloping horses can be seen. But the most striking point is the variety of the representations given by the sculptor.

Female Head. 2nd – 3rd century. Toprak-Kala. The Hermitage. St Petersburg.

Megalithic art

Megalithic statues, called balbaly, knew a great expansion over the huge territory that extended from northern Mongolia to the steppes of southern Russia, conquered by the Turks during the 6th and 7th century. The conception underlying the building of megalithic monuments is still unknown. They are considered the incarnation of a dead spirit, an ancestor or even the representation of a vanquished enemy. Their aspect is extremely simple: a flat roofing slab is put on top of a high block of stone, a head and hands half-crossed are roughly hewn. Sometimes one hand holds a vase. The line of the face with slit eyes as well as some details of their costumes is very stylized. The only indication allowing us to determine the sex of the character is a moustache for the men and round breasts for the women. They are impassible idols whose plasticity is generalized to the extreme, but paradoxically, it gives them a very great expressiveness. The megalithic monuments are in harmony to an astonishing degree with the monotonous scenery of the steppes.

Figurines

Baked clay figurines, sculptures, or reliefs of small dimensions were known in Central Asia since the Neolithic epoch and the Bronze Age (2nd and 4th millennium before our era). In this faraway epoch numerous baked clay statuettes were totemic representations of livestock breeders. Some roughly represented domestic animals. Others were related to the cult of farming. Among them, the statuette of a goddess was particularly popular. Its cult goes back to the matriarchal period.

Archaeologists in the South of Turkmenistan have discovered entire collections of carved statuettes of this goddess. During the Neolithic period the sculpture in round bosse predominated. During the Bronze Age, stylization began to exploit volume, the forms became more conventional, the chests were hardly silhouetted. Much meaning was given to the headdress. In this epoch representations of men linked to the rite of fecundity and nature renewal also appeared, but were less frequent. The conventional characteristic of the general forms remained the same.

Around the beginning of the first millenium before our era, the baked clay figurines gradually disappeared in Central Asia for reasons that aren't yet clear. However the great goddess cult seems to have taken roots in the popular conscience. The first century before our era gave a new impetus to the design of the baked clay figurines. This impulse corresponds to the introduction in

Central Asia of statuettes executed in Hellenistic western countries. The direct copy of the Greek models was observed only in a small number of baked clay sculptures (Athena wearing a helmet, Medusa's head, a bearded Silenus mask with a bald skull). Local artistic traditions predominated in numerous variations which have survived and can now be seen in various museums. During this epoch the statuettes were, for a great part, realised with the help of a mould. Very often they were covered with a red coating, a colour that had a particular meaning in Eastern aesthetics and beliefs. The principal goddesses' figurines of the local pantheon had a privileged place.

Divine Warrior, 6th – 7th century.
The Art History Institute. Tashkent.

Toy Dragon. 20th century. Fine Arts
Museum of the Uzbekistan Republic.
Tashkent.

The naked figurines, full length and full face, the arms along the body or with a hand on the breast and the other on the womb are related to the mother-goddess. The statuettes of goddesses draped in long garments, Greek style, were all the fashion until our era. They are considerably different according to their regional origins and reflect the particularities of their ethnic surroundings: the lines of the faces, the headgear, and the cult attributes. The goddesses are represented full length or sitting down. Nearly all these works have in common the same frontal representation, a schematisation of the face devoid of all expression, and rich garments. Across the centuries the style of the statuettes underwent some changes. The more ancient ones were of baked clay executed in relief, with lithe drapery and bodies in proportion to the head. During the first centuries the aspect of the goddesses changes. The head in high relief is of an excessive size in regard to the torso which is cut in flat dalle. The drapery is rigid, almost linear. The dresses are adorned with local elements, the heavy downs made in thick material are often enhanced with ornamental appliqué; sometimes a cape covers the shoulders.

A new approach of the artists in the creation of types is responsible for these changes. In high antiquity the sculptures were trying to express the divinity by an ideal beauty and they gave the goddesses the appearance of a beautiful and majestic woman. Later on, they privileged a conventional figure, a divinity who excluded the possibility to establish a comparison with a real feminine beauty, thus giving to the goddesses an abstract, timeless character. The male statuettes in the ancient sculpture of Central Asia are less numerous. From the 2nd and 1st century A.D., figurines of horsemen became popular. Their appearance is probably linked to traditions of the semi-nomads' world to which belong the Arsacids, the Kushan monarchs and the Kangui Governors before they entered into history; the representations of horsemen are part of urban culture. They were roughly modelled by hand and their aspect deliberately lacks finish. The nose is flat, the mouth is a hole, the eyes are marked by a split or pastillage. The original idols are probably linked to the primitive beliefs of nomad people and the magic capacity of this deity to drive away bad spirits.

During the 3rd century a new type of baked clay sculpture appeared at Merv: a man with royal headgear, curly hair and a beard, wearing a rich kaftan and baggy trousers, leaning on a sword. According to his iconography this individual is close to the majestic figures of the Persian monarchs of the Sassanid and their Governors. But it is improbable that he represents a real person. It rather seems that he came out of the Khorassan legends.

The so-called Dionysiac sculptures probably belong to the cycle of the

Toy whistles. 20th century. Fine Arts Museum of the Uzbekistan Republic. Tashkent.

Fantastic creatures, toys. 20th century. Museum of Archaeology, History and the Fine Arts. Dusanbe.

popular theatrical feasts that went with the monumental sculpture. The musician figures tell us about their instruments and give us precious information about musical culture in Central Asia. There are also some figurines of disguised people, actors and dancers. A baked clay figure from Kharezm represents a half-naked figure holding a knife to cut the grapes and with a grape in his hand.

The statuettes of animals are also numerous: horses, sheep, camels. They are modelled by hand and the forms and proportions are respected. The details in the shape of the head or the entire figures incorporated on cassolettes used for the cult and on certain vases, obviously testify to the ritual significance of these representations.

During the 4th and 5th century, figures of demonic creatures with rough faces, eyes staring out of their sockets and grimacing mouths were numerous. These magical representations are intensively expressive. During troubled war periods the protective genius must have given hope to anxious men and conjured away misfortune.

During the early Middle Ages the baked clay figurines were found throughout Sogdian until Islam put an end to them. The baked clay figures of the 6th and 7th century coming, for example, from Samarkand are striking by the diversity of the people and the ethnic types depicted. Women's heads are crowned with flowers and jewels. But different form the older baked clay figures, the representations of men, mainly bearded riders of Turkish or Sogdian type, holding bludgeons in their hands dominated this entire period. Young men wear headgear resembling a crown, with wings or a crescent moon. These artistically perfect heads are often endowed with a small body naively fashioned with small bits of clay imitating torso and crossed arms.

During the Islamic period the representation of men in baked clay in Central Asia disappeared almost entirely and didn't reappear until the 12th and 14th century. But at the same time the figurines of animals (real or imaginary) lost their ritual significance and were only used as toys.

Figurines of this kind were executed in great numbers during the pre-Revolutionary period and these traditions have lived on in the work of popular artists in Uzbekistan and Tadjikistan even today...

Ossuaries

Ossuaries constitute a particular domain of small sculpture. Like little coffins in baked clay or plaster, according to the Avesta prescriptions, they were used for the bones of the dead. Some of them are adorned with small figurines made with moulds.

In Ancient Kharezm, ossuaries were represented in a standard way: the women figures are sitting (rarely standing); the men have thick eyebrows, long noses and pointed beards. Sometimes they wear a large brimmed hat and baggy trousers and a narrow kaftan. On these ossuaries the women have a neatly drawn profile. Their hair falls on their back in a braid. They wear a close-fitting dress. Their breasts are hardly indicated and their hips are broad. It is possible that they represent old Kharezm gods from the living world as well as the world of the dead.

Cold and impassible, these sculptures at the same time closely resemble the inhabitants of Kharezm. The stylized bodies and faces are extremely expressive and reflect a divine renouncement. On a certain number of ossuaries from the region of Merv, we can see either whimpers or heads moulded with the help of a matrice, but each time representing an identical type: long face, stamped with sadness, regular lines, eyes turned towards the sky and opened mouth.

The ossuaries of the region situated in the east of Samarkand are of a particular group. They are rectangular, bordered with a notched motif and have a pyramidal cover. The four faces of the casket are decorated with low relief presenting a similar composition. One of them is decorated by an arch way with curved columns between which stand women and men holding various objects: the men, sacred fires, cooks with snakes' heads, pokers; the women plants, a big key, a crown, an ossuary. They are probably priests and priestesses holding ritual objects and celebrating a ceremony concerning fire and funeral rites.

The ossuaries from Molla-Kurgan (Uzbekistan) and the old town of Krasnoretchenski (Kirghizstan), are original in their decoration showing an altar where a flame burned, flanked by two priests holding pokers and something to be burnt. This kind of ossuary belongs to the period of the early Middle Ages in Sogdian art.

The revival of independant art

Following centuries of apathy, sculpture as an independent form of art was only revived after the October Revolution. The old traditions are alive in the work of a great number of modern sculptors who followed the example of a panel of Tadjik Akhunov entitled *The Ribbon Dance*. This low-relief in copper executed au repoussé represents young girls dancing among spectators. The dancers' figures, their poses, recall the caryatids of Pendjikent by their exaggeratedly thin waists. The absence of relief which characterized this panel repeats the low-reliefs in wood of Pendjikent and Kalai-Kakhkakh and the applied art of the 6th and 7th century.

In his work *Hospitality*, the sculptor Khabibuline takes his inspiration from another artistic epoch. He represents a young Kirghized girl whose straight face and figure recall megalithic sculptures. Even though her face is impassible, as required by national etiquette, she looks affable. The forms of her body, although very schematic, depict a juvenile grace. The cup she holds in her hand is not a ritual attribute but a cup of fresh koumys, that she presents to a host or a tired traveller. Here, the sculptor gives a new view of humanity to an ancient plastic representation bringing it a humanitarian vision of the 20th century world.

The potters Omar Djourakoulov of Samarkand, Gafour Khalilov of Ura-Tube, Khamro Rakhimov of Bukhara have executed several hundreds of baked clay works, among which some very expressive dragons, fantastic birds, horses designed with naive humour. In these works, primitive plasticity united with rich fantasy gives an astonishing attraction to all these objects.

In recent years professional sculptors have shaped a new type of baked clay statue, profoundly national in spirit and modern in theme. A. Moukhtarov of Samarkand has crated a series of compositions in which scenes of everyday life and people are represented with a humour full of kindness, characteristic of Central Asian folklore.

Dance with Ribbons, panel, 1976.
O. Akhounouv. Public Library Firdusi, Dusanbe.

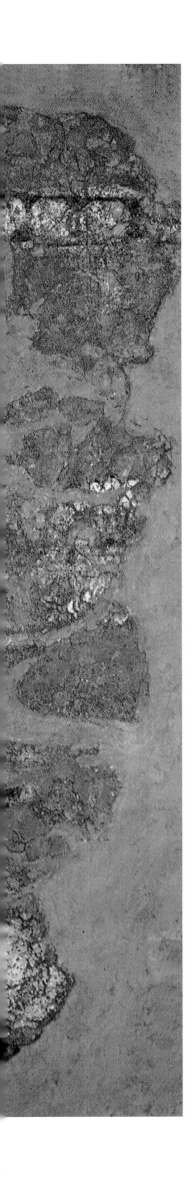

MONUMENTAL PAINTING AND ILLUMINATION

The painting in Central Asia goes back several millennia. The rocks drawings of Zaraoutsai (south of Uzbekistan) date from the Palaeolithic age and the mural painting of Pessedjikdepe (south of Turkmenistan), from the Neolithic age. But they are only isolated examples of a very ancient history of this art in the vast territory of Central Asia.

Carriers of Offerings. 7th century.
Fragment from a mural painting of
Adjina-tépé. The Hermitage,
St Petersburg.

Monumental painting

Mural painting spread widely during antiquity and the Middle Ages. It was, then, tightly linked with architecture which predetermined its stylistic particularities to a great extent: the absence of any model and the monumental character of the forms, the combination of figurative and ornamental elements, the local colours encircled by red and black. At the same time, the painting maintained its own artistic vocation, expressing social ideas and aesthetic ideals of the historical and cultural centres where it was produced. Ancient painting came to us in fragments and it is difficult to judge the subjects of its compositions. However it can be said with certainty that the paintings' themes are extremely varied: no fragment recently discovered repeats a subject already treated.

Painting became increasingly prevalent during the 2nd and 3rd century and evolved; characteristic traits were observed. But Barbarian tribes who occupied the region forced art back toward more primitive forms.

It was then necessary to wait until the 3rd century was animated by a new breath. While respecting tradition, painting began to open to new forms and new ideals.

The painting of the early Middle Ages (6th and 7th century) is an extremely astonishing phenomenon in the history of world art. The Sogdian frescos in the palace of Varakhcha and Aphrasiab, in the numerous private houses, palaces and temples of Pendjikent, the paintings of the Usrushan, neighbouring region to Sogdian, the Buddhist mural paintings on the territory of the ancient Bactrian at Kalai-Kafirnigan testify to the existence of a particular school of monumental painting formed if not as a corporation, at least as a group of highly qualified professional artists.

Painting remains traditional in the monasteries and Buddhist sanctuaries but Hindu canons become more and more considerable.

Ambassadors Bearing Gifts. 7th century. Fragment of mural painting in Aphrasiab palace. The Uzbekistan Museum of Art History and Culture in Samarkand.

Head of a Warrior, 6th – 7th century.
Detail of mural painting in Aphrasiab
palace. Museum of History of the
Peoples of Uzbekistan. Tashkent.

Four-armed goddess riding a lion.
7-8th century. Fragments of a Kala-
kakh-kakh mural painting.
The Hermitage. St Petersburg.

The Buddha faces of Adjina-tépé are represented slightly turned toward the
faithful. The Buddhas are positioned in arches forming iconostases. They are
set one near the other or above one another. As for the Buddhists holding
offerings, they are very different: the painter borrowed his models from real
life and painted them in a somewhat summary manner. The faces are outlined
with a rich and exact line, slender figures, garment folds, attributes. The faces
are represented in profile or three quarters. All the personages are set in relief
against a red background. The profane themes know a blossoming without
equal in painting, in the Sogdian and Usrushan regions. Far from representing
scenes of current life, painting takes its inspiration from more elaborate
subjects suggested by epic legends, myths, moral fables and popular tales. It
represents banquets, scenes of battle or hunting games with noblemen,
warriors, ladies from the contemporary surrounding of the painter, who also
adds fantastic beings and divinities from the local pantheon.

Palace frescos

The paintings which adorn the walls of Varakhcha and Aphrasiab palaces are solemn in their contents and monumental in their style.

The paintings of the throne hall in the palace of Varakhcha celebrate the royal power.

In the centre of the principal wall is the monumental figure of the king. His throne is supported by winged camels.

On both sides real life imposes itself to the glance. The king is performing legal proceedings; his wife and the heir are burning sacred plants in a deep cassolette.

On the other walls are painted scenes of battle, hunting or entertainment. Altogether they conform to the real ceremonies of the court, to the religious rites, to the feasts given in the palace. The scenes are represented in an epic form. On the four walls of the large Red Hall, heroes mounted on an elephant are fighting against cheetahs and griffons.

Buddhist engravings of the 8th century.

Mural paintings from Bezeklik,
7th – 10th century.

Composition with several people.
1st century. Fresco fragment.
Art History Institute. Tashkent.

The drawing in the painting at Varakhcha is harmonious; it transmits the plasticity of the figures and their movements, but the forms are treated in flat tint. Attentive study allows us to see that the final drawing is traced by means of a black or red line, not corresponding, in a great many cases, to the general line of the sketch. In all probability, the painter introduced corrections during his work. The frescos of the principal halls of the noble palaces at Samarkand, as well as at Aphrasiab, make a vivid impression. The compositions of each wall glorify the dynasty of the royal family. They also reflect real events but, here too, in an epic interpretation. One of the scenes presents a rich nuptial procession, a princess escorted by a cavalcade and servants holding the wedding presents. Another one presents the king of Samarkand receiving ambassadors coming from their different countries, holding presents in their arms. On the third wall a boat can be seen in which stands a young Chinese girl being conducted, probably, to the harem of a nobleman. On the river's banks horsemen fight wild beasts. Only a few details of the painting have been preserved. All the frescos distinguished themselves by an elegant research in the drawing, which allow us to think that artists of a very high level worked in the studios of the capital of Sogdian. What distinguishes the Sogdian mural paintings of the 6th-8th century is that they decorate not only the palaces and places dedicated to the cult, but also the private houses of the town's inhabitants. At Pendjikent a full gallery of paintings can be seen, and one may be astonished by the great number of artists working in this small town. The multiplicity of styles and the artistic process, the infinite diversity of the compositions which never repeated themselves, even for identical subjects, are also very striking. The scenes represented are the illustrations of epic episodes taken from different tales. Among the mythological characters a particular role is devoted to a goddess with four arms, sitting on a snake or a lion, or seeming to emerge from the clouds. There are also a masculine divinity with a solar disc and a feminine divinity with a blue lunar disc. But they are only simple figurants in a composition with multiple personages where men play the principal roles. Numerous compositions relate the exploits of valorous warriors riding sometimes at the head of an army, sometimes alone against an enemy or a dragon. It is supposed that these scenes illustrate the legends of the invincible warrior, Roustam. The scenes of banquets or tournaments, battles and hunts are particularly expressive. All this confers an epic valour on real events and does not at all romanticize life at the beginning of the feudal epoch. The painters often found their inspiration in popular tales or fables, such the tale, known over all the territory from ancient Greece to India, about a goose that laied golden eggs and was killed by its stupid master to make a succulent meal. The artistic language of Pendjikent is rich and varied. The

palette is sometimes saturated, at other times shadowed in half tone. The battle scenes are full of dramatic tension or built on a quaint rhythm. The subjects drawn from court life respect etiquette, the mythological subjects combine fantasy and reality into a harmonious whole. By the Islamic epoch ornaments were already important in the mural painting of Central Asia. Representations of living creatures are sometimes present in the pictorial decoration of palaces. Fragments of these paintings have recently been discovered in an edifice from the 10th century at Khulbuk. We know that at the end of the 14th century and beginning of the 15th century, the palaces of Tamerlan at Samarkand were decorated with paintings about subjects illustrating warriors' exploits and palace life. They were the conqueror's, his wife's, son's and grandson's portraits. The painting of the Abd-a-Aziz-Khan madrasah at Bukhara (17th century) are somewhat unusual. Architectural landscapes with pavilions among trees are depicted in a style influenced by Indian paintings of the epoch of the Great Moguls. But these are rare exceptions in monumental painting, where purely decorative motives predominate.

Procession of ambassadors. 7th century. Mural painting in Aphrasiab palace. The Uzbekistan Museum of Art History and Culture in Samarkand.

Scene from the Tale of the Goose.
6th – 7th century. Detail, Pendjikent
mural painting.
The Hermitage. St Petersburg.

93

Farkhad and the Stone-Cutters.
Khamse of Navoi miniature,
1521-1522. Saltykov-Chtchedrine
Public Library. St Petersburg.

Flight of the Sultan Mohammed
Bokhadur-Khan, Fatkh-Nameh
miniature. 16th century.
Institute of Oriental Studies of the
Academy of Sciences in Uzbekistan.
Tashkent.

A Young Beauty and an Old Man.
Tuhfat ul-Akhrar de Djâmi, c. 1570.
Saltykov-Chtchedrine public library.
St Petersburg.

Illumination

From the 14th and 15th century onwards, miniature painting was prevalent. The manuscripts of the Muslim Orient constitute a specific branch of the arts. Their fabrication took long months of assiduous work, carried out by the calligraphers and artists who took charge of the ornamentation using water-colours heightened with gold. The illuminations covered a full sheet and the margins done by the copyist were particularly refined. Even though the manuscripts were ordered by the higher social class, the miniatures were mostly the expression of the popular concept of "beauty", considering that those who made them descended from lower classes. An Oriental writer of the 15th century mentions that many artists worked in Tamerlan's palace in Samarkand. The most famous one was Abd al-Hadji, a miniaturist from Baghdad. Seeing that he was a master of illumination, one can draw the conclusion that the other artists he directed were also miniaturists. Amongst the enormous heritage constituted by the miniatures of the times of the

Timurides in the 14th and 15th century, the difficulty we meet if we want to highlight the art works of Central Asia can be justified by the fact that very few works were actually signed. Even when miniature-embellished manuscripts indicated the exact locality of provenance, that didn't necessarily mean that the illustrators belonged to the artistic school of the region mentioned; their attribution however is made easier by the following indications: the Oriental miniaturists (like the painters of western Europe in those days) illustrating an historical or literary text, drew inspiration from their habitual environment, introducing architecture and everyday objects around them. Local ethnic features were also given to characters who were represented by the costumes of a particular country and period. The Timurides of Mavera-un-nahr, for instance, orientated themselves mostly towards the surroundings of Turkmenistan in Central Asia. This explains why the characters in their miniatures wear clothes, hairstyles, shoes and other details in accordance with this context.

Following page:
The Lovers. Saadi Bustan miniature. 16th century. Saltykov-Chtchedrine Public Library. St Petersburg.

Gazankhan in Urdjaine. Tariklu Abulkhaire miniature. 16th century. Institute of Oriental Studies of the Academy of Sciences in Uzbekistan. Tashkent.

Styles

Two stylistic orientations distinguish the miniatures of the 15th and 16th century. One could be defined as "romantic", the other as "narrative". If the first one distinguishes itself through meticulous composition, refined drawing and rich colour for lyrical and dramatic subjects, the second one is characterized by control and terseness of artistic procedures and a more important neutrality concerning the choice of subjects and the serene balance of composition. These two tendencies are found in the illustrations of Shah-Nameh (*The Book of Kings*), probably created throughout the 15th century; art historians relate it to the school of Central Asia. The illustrations were made by two miniaturists. One of them preferred dramatically loaded subjects: heroes fighting, their struggle against demons, the bird Simurgh taking a child away to the mountains, Siavouch enduring the ordeal by fire... These miniatures are painted with much refinement; the figures are small, the scenery is romantic, the colours are warm and the volumes take shape by means of colour. The second illustrator preferred genre painting. He depicted royal receptions, the construction of ramparts, the trade of the blacksmith, the trying on of clothes. His figures are bigger and their treatment is more detailed. The background is neutral. The colours are local, saturated, applied with regular coats. The art of miniature painting in Central Asia distinguishes itself by very elaborated representation of stereotypes. Seen from this angle, it is close to Oriental poetry, which has created and maintained its well defined metaphors and poetical allegories over the centuries. For instance, the "slender cypress" (or poplar tree) evokes a beautiful young girl, "bow and arrows", her eyebrows and look of irresistible charm, the "pearls", her white teeth, but the "pearls" also stand for a flight of poetic words (one could infinitely prolong these metaphorical examples). This "poetry of allusion" is also present in the art of the miniature. Allegorical expressions can be found in all miniatures. The artists introduced them in manuscripts of literary, historical and scientific natures, and they sometimes didn't even coincide with the contents of a particular episode within the illustrated work. The second-rate miniaturists contented themselves with copying faithfully, whereas the painters of a very high level added a personal interpretation, often creating entirely new compositions. During the second decade of the 16th century after having escaped Herat of the Timurides, artists found refuge in Central Asia, a brilliant cultural centre in those days. The miniaturists who accompanied them discovered a favourable terrain there, with many already flourishing traditions. Bukhara became the main centre of this artistic activity, but miniatures were also created in the palaces of art patrons of other important cities like Samarkand and Shakhruakhia (near Tashkent). The miniatures of this period were based on the traditions of two schools: the local school of Mavera-un-nahr and the school of Herat linked with the great miniaturist Kemaleddine Behzad.

Experts Discussing Hunting. Miniature in the Book of Ilkhan's Hunts. 17th century. Institute of Oriental Studies of the Academy of Sciences in Uzbekistan. Tashkent.

The schools

The distinctive features of narrative style are revealed in the miniatures of the only tome of a poem called *Fatkh-Nameh* (early 16th century): precise drawing but without emotion, large figures but few, well-balanced and static compositions. This severe style, without any details, using restrained colour, gives the miniatures of *Fatkh-Nameh* their great originality. The local Uzbekan element is present in the aspect of the characters, in their clothing; their surrounding environment denotes their ancient nomadic traditions.

This local aspect is characteristic of many miniatures of the first half of the 16th century, outstanding because of the remarkable mastery of their painting. That is what the illustrations of Khamsé d'Alciher Navoï, copied out and illustrated in *Shakhruakhia* by two miniaturists, are like. The first compositions are slightly static, with few characters, big and strong figures, the drawing fine and precise. The colours are well-matched, but the palette has its limitations and the colours are condensed and without gloss. The colours of the second illustrator are more vivid; the compositions are more complex and dynamic, the figures slimmer and their movements more fluid. Miniatures which embellish the *Anvari-Sukheili* by the poet Kachifi are very close to the former ones mentioned as far as their style is concerned, but their manner is more intimate.

The artist chooses genre scenes evolving in the heart of nature. The figures are graceful, their movements lithe; they stand out against the background of hills studded with tufts of grass, or a golden sky flecked with fleecy clouds. The compositions are based on the contrast between the undulating lines of the hills and the figures expressed in brief outlines.

The details of Uzbek clothing and objects furnishing the interiors are represented in the miniatures of the *History of Aboulkhaïr*, independently of the characters, Alexander the Great or Sassanid shahs. The nomadic lifestyle of the steppes predominates in depicting the environment. The most frequent subject of these miniatures is a reception by the khan, taking place according to the strict rules of étiquette, not in a palace, but in the middle of nature amongst tents and yurts. The compositions are rather static; the range of colours is bright and contrasting. The landscape is usually treated in a decorative manner.

Siavouch Undergoing Trial by Fire.
Firdusi Scha-Nameh miniature.
17th century.
Institute of Oriental Studies of the
Academy of Sciences in
Uzbekistan.Tashkent.

The modern miniaturists and their successors

In the 17th century, a mutual exchange of artistic techniques between artists of Central Asia and India is evident. In works by Avaz Muhammad and Mullo Behzad one can discern characteristic traits of Hindu miniatures, like relief of the figures, distancing levels by using perspective, the introduction of typical Hindu details of everyday life in the composition.

In the beginning of the 18th century, the art of the miniature disappeared almost entirely, and the creation of illustrated manuscripts ceased completely during the second half of the 19th century, as the printed book became widespread in Turkestan and in the Transcaspian provinces.

The renaissance of thematic painting in Central Asia only came about in the 20th century. The rich archaeological discoveries of monumental painting dating back as far as the pre-Islamic period have given the modern painters the opportunity to get in touch with ancient pictorial traditions. This heritage has proven to be extremely fruitful for many artists. We can cite as an example the paintings of Tchinguiz Akhmarov based on the theme of the Sogdian wedding decorating the café of the resting area of the cable factory in Tashkent, where the workmen organized meetings and family celebrations. The painter drew inspiration from works of Aphrasiab and Pendjikent. The composition, which covers three walls, is painted in golden shades combining here and there with strokes of vivid blue.

The ancient painting of Central Asia will probably continue to interest modern painters, who for the moment draw more inspiration from the miniaturists. Among these contemporary artists are monumentalists, easel-painters, masters of etching in black and in colour.

Tchinguiz Akhmarov is one of the most promising artists in this context. He remains attached to the miniature traditions of the Institute of Oriental Studies, the Institute of Art History (Tashkent), the Museum of Ulug-Beg (Samarkand) and many other edifices. The Navoï poems represent the subject of his paintings; allegories about the arts, life and tragic death of Ulug-Beg, caravans from faraway countries, popular celebrations...

The painter remains demanding as far as the choice of his subjects are concerned and will always try to attain a close correspondence between the content and the style of his paintings.

Fighting between the Persians and the Turanians. Zafar-Nameh miniature. 17th century. Institute of Oriental Studies of the Academy of Sciences in Uzbekistan. Tashkent.

بجهافعت و مقاتله ء دشمنان دست جلادت برکشاد ند د چون کوه پای نبات قتردم کوشتهاء مردانه نمود ند و مرجند سپاه مخالف بد و یکدیکر یرسیدند و بنیزه و شمشر و سالین حمله می آور دند اشان بزخم تبرزمه را باز مسکر دانید ند ها تزنگ کمان کرده جانهاستو فنافش کنان تیر بر برکر و ه ها تا جهانشاه بهادر با نومان حود از طرفی دیکر د رامد و بر دشمنان حمله آور ده جنگ

در پیوست

THE DECORATIVE ARTS

Ceramics

Ceramics are the most traditional form of decorative arts in Central Asia.

The oldest centres of civilisation on the territory of today's Turkmenistan: Kara-tépé, Gheoksiour, Ak-dépé, Altyne-dépé, Namasga-dépé, dating from the 4th - 2nd millennium B.C., have provided us with remarkable specimens of painted pottery of the archaic type. The appearance of the potter's wheel and the firing of pottery in the kiln at the end of the 3rd - beginning of the 2nd millennium B.C. can be considered as a kind of technological revolution which resulted in great diversity of pottery forms and their decorative principles.

At that time, painted ceramics spread widely on the huge territory of the Oriental world, from Mesopotamia to India.

Throughout the first part of the 1st millennium B.C., the traditions of painting gradually disappeared, but the beauty and perfection of form in ceramics persisted.

Vase, bowl and jug. 1st – 2nd century.
Art History Institute. Tashkent.

Antiquity

The potters of antiquity (3rd century B.C. - 4th century) attained a high level making ceramic objects. During the first centuries of our era in the regions of North Central Asia, the decoration of recipients became widespread, mostly of small-sized jugs, decorated with zoomorphic miniatures which were claimed to have a protective role: they were linked with the art of cattle breeding tribes and the practice of their cults.

The ritual torches frorm the south of Tadjikistan and Uzbekistan bear witness to the enlargement of thematic possibilities of antique ceramics. Thus, the torchholder discovered in Saksonokhour (1st century) has shapes of birdheads and animals; another one from Khaltchayan (1st century B.C.) is decorated with figures of stylized men. Ancient crockery is extremely varied. The dishes for banquets are elegant and solemn; the jugs, pots and bowls are distinguished by the simplicity of their form. Many of them have been discovered on the sites of old Bactrian towns, Sogdian and Marghiane. The dishes, bowls and vases were covered with a thick; red earthy coating and the jugs with a light coating. The specimens of ancient ceramics of Central Asia allow us to comprehend the links they establish with Persian artistic traditions, and those of ancient Greece and nomadic tribes of the north.

Water holder. 7th – 8th century. Fine Arts Museum of the Uzbekistan Republic. Tashkent.

Bowl with geometric pattern. 4000-3000 B.C. Historical Museum of the Turkmenistan Repub ic. Achkhabad.

Ladle. 3rd – 4th century. Ethnographical Institute of the Academy of Sciences. Moscow.

Dish. 10th century. The Uzbekistan
Museum of Art History and Culture in
Samarkand.

Dish with the inscription 'Barakat'
(happiness). 11th century.

The Middle Ages

In the beginning of the Middle Ages the heritage of antiquity was still alive, even though new decorative forms and solutions were developing. The ewers or *mourgoba* (literally "waterbird") are quite original with their stylized bird shape, placed on a small hollow pedestal like a flattened cone. On one of the ewers, dating from the 12th century and discovered in Kuva (Ferghana), the neck ends in the shape of a wild boar.

The unglazed ceramics of the 9th and 12th century are represented by high jugs, flat flasks, small bowls and cups decorated with animals, birds and even men from time to time, in spite of the banning of graphic representations of living creatures by Islam. This decoration was engraved.

Engraved crockery was made in many towns of Mavera-un-nahr, Kharezm and Ferghana. The ornamentation of recipients from Merv in the 12th century is particularly rich: gray bowls with a delicate inside surface, small jugs with large necks of which the outside decoration seems to be woven. Their bellies were made of two halves cast on moulds and glued together afterwards. The designs of the decoration are extremely varied: plant shoots with fantastic tangles that form a background with bunting scenes, medallions with supernatural creatures: a winged sphinx with a woman's face, birds with men's heads, mermaids and harpies. Their artistic interpretation is true to the folk nature of these representations.

The decorative style of these objects is based on the repetition of the rhythmical character of ornamental patterns. Epigraphic decorations appeared as well at the beginning of the Islamic period.

In between the 9th and the 12th century, painted ceramic crockery of the archaic style, embellished mainly with foliage resembling the traditional islimi adornment, was developed in the towns and in the countryside of the whole of Central Asia.

Jug. 7th – 8th century.
The Hermitage. St Petersburg.

Starting from the 9th century, and throughout the following centuries, glazed ceramics attained a quality close to artistic perfection. Jugs, vases, large-sized dishes were covered with plan-like epigraphic and sometimes zoomorphic elements. Often several kinds of adornments were used on the same object. From the 9th until the beginning of the 13th century, the city Aphrasiab in Samarkand was considered as one of the centres of glazed ceramics in Central Asia. The objects coming from Aphrasiab are distinguished by the quality of their materials, glaze and colour, and the absolute perfection of shape and decoration. The high standard of decorative objects attained in the 9th and 10th century suggests that throughout this period there were not only master turners, but also a special category of painters and decorators. The potters of Samarkand, assimilating the decorative technology of underglaze or overglaze, accomplished remarkable results as far as decorative possibilities of colour are concerned. The first attempts of stylizing adornment and inscriptions took place in the 9th and 10th century with the decoration of glazed ceramics. This type of ceramic from the regions of Merv, Nissa, Chach, Ferghana, Tchaganian and Semiretchie has achieved celebrity. In these regions, the decoration of objects is predominated by a range of olive-green highlighted with brown, yellow and ochre-red. The ornamental list contains animals, birds and fish which reflect local symbolism and folk traditions. The iconography of certain images was taken from the art of engraving vocabulary of the beginning of the Middle Ages.

In the 13th and 14th century, after the invasion of Gengis Khan, the historiated designs of the glazed ceramic decoration made way for stylized plant designs, while geometrical and zoomorphic figures were used only rarely. Almost everywhere the colours changed abruptly.

Jug. Historical Museum of the Kirghiz
Republic. Frunze.

Dish. 10th – 11th century.

The polychrome style of the 9th and 12th century generated a more graphic style through drawing and a less emotional style because of the blue ceramic colour on black decorations, underglaze or black adornments, azure blue and deep blue, contrasting with a white background.

The development of the glazed ceramics underwent a new development at the end of the 14th - early 15th century. As a consequence of the important economical and commercial links maintained by the Kingdom of the Timurides with other countries, a new type of ceramic imitating the imported Chinese porcelain was introduced in Central Asia in the 15th century. These silicate-based ceramics were produced in a number of towns: Bukhara, Chakhri-Siabz, Merv, Nissa, Urgench, but the main centre was Samarkand. The glazed dishes of Samarkand with blue decorations on a milky white background are specimens of this type of ceramic, at a time when artists were looking for their own decorative solutions and refused to copy foreign models. In those days, the craftsmen who made glazed crockery also produced tiles intended for covering buildings, with colour that was surprisingly stable and intense.

Jug. 12th century.

Jug. 11th – 12th century.

Modern times

In the beginning of the 16th century, ceramics still pursued the traditions of the previous century, but in the beginning of the 17th century, cobalt-blue, very expensive because imported, was replaced by colouring of inferior quality, and silicate was replaced by clay. These changes reflect the general aspect of ceramic crockery in the 17th and 18th century: it is less refined and its inside surface is thicker.

Glazed ceramics of the 19th and early 20th century attained less perfection than they had throughout the 9th and 16th century, but the simplicity of their shapes and the glossy joyful ornamentation confers great originality on these objects. The decoration remained traditional, based on plant and geometrical designs; in the middle of the 19th century, painted subjects representing simple objects were added on the large round dishes: teapots, guns and knifes. And still today, the traditional ceramic works have a considerable importance in everyday life of the people in Central Asia.

Metals

The artistic work concerning metals is influenced by the arts of bordering regions. Nevertheless, the works produced in Central Asia have unquestionably great originality. The unity of style of the art of engraving is noticeable at almost every stage of its development, even though the particularities of each local school are preserved.

Jug. 12th century.

Dish. 19th century. History Museum
of the Peoples of Uzbekistan.
Tashkent.

Bronze cauldron decorated with goats
in high relief . 6th – 4th century B.C.
History Museum of the Peoples of
Uzbekistan. Tashkent.

Cassolette. 5th-3rd century B.C.
Historical Museum of the Kirghiz
Republic. Frunze.

Previous pages:
Tray. 11th – 12th century.
The Hermitage. St Petersburg.

Tray with the name of the shah
Kharezm Abu Ibrahim. 11th – 12th
century.

Handled ewer decorated with a band
of pomegranates. 12th century.
History Museum of the Peoples of
Uzbekistan. Tashkent.

The Middle Ages

The art of engraving in antiquity and the early Middle Ages is principally represented by gilded silver crockery and, less frequently, works in gold. Starting from the 11th century, in Central Asia and the Near and Middle East the metals mostly used were copper and its alloys.

The fasteners or bronze brooches embellished with zoomorphic designs, and sometimes little genre scenes, widely used at the end of the 3rd - beginning of the 2nd millennium in the regions of the Mediterranean, Mesopotamia, Egypt and India, were still very much influenced by the ancient Oriental civilizations.

The works of the 6th and 4th century B.C. were closely linked with the "animal style" of the Sakas and the Scythians, of which the appearance was particularly important in the north and east of Central Asia. The numerous objects made of bronze in those days were embellished with supernatural and true to life animal representations and hunting scenes with wild animals. This particular style often came from the artist's desire to depict the animal, by generalizing its shape and stripping it of all unnecessary details. This terseness gave the works an astonishing artistic integrity. The animal figurines edging ritual cauldrons, embellishing altars, censers and pommels of daggers or the images in relief with an openwork design of griffins, ibexes, horses on plates, buckles, and other ornamental pieces prove that to us.

Dish. 12th century. The Uzbekistan Museum of Art History and Culture in Samarkand.

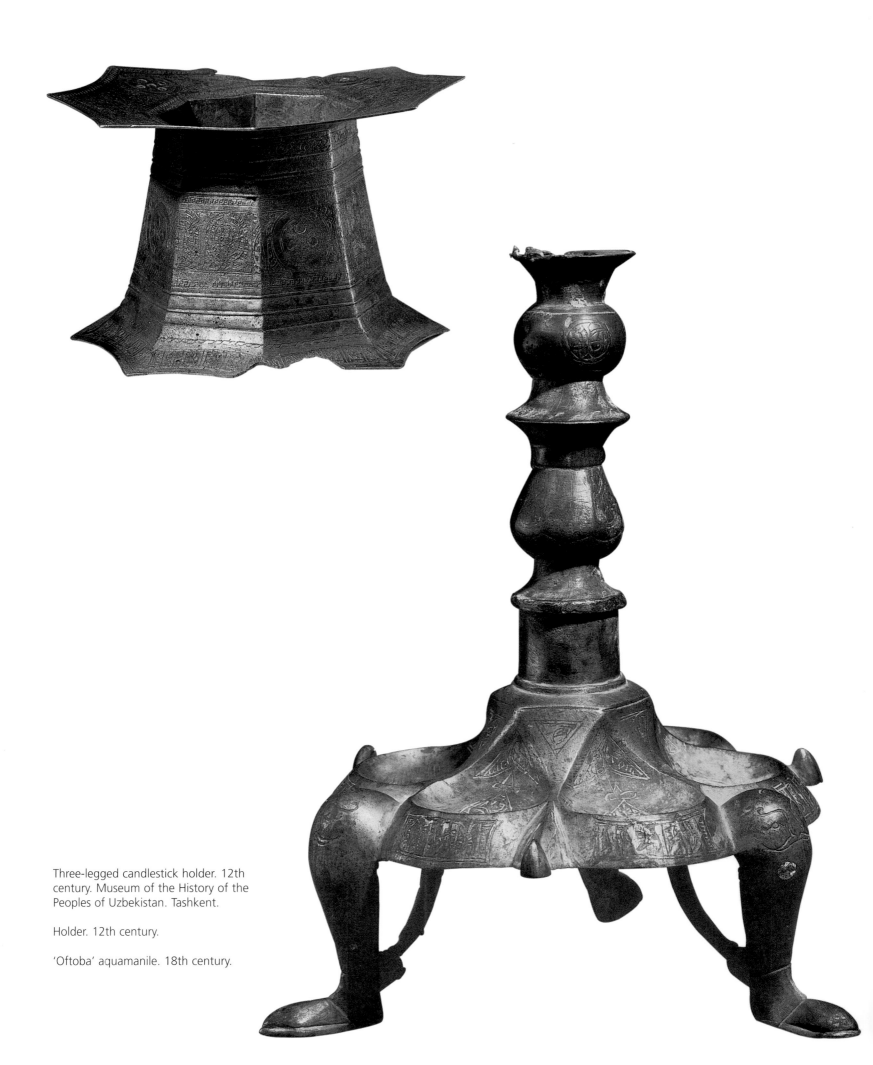

Three-legged candlestick holder. 12th century. Museum of the History of the Peoples of Uzbekistan. Tashkent.

Holder. 12th century.

'Oftoba' aquamanile. 18th century.

'Oftoba' aquamanile and 'tschoidiche'
ewer. 19th century. Museum of the
History of the Peoples of Uzbekistan.
Tashkent.

The art of engraving of Tokharistan

The art of engraving of Tokharistan is profoundly influenced by the traditions of Hellenistic art, particularly valued by the Bactrian craftsmen from days before the Kushans. A silver ceremonial vase embellished with a large frieze in relief, on which scenes of a drama by Euripides take place, is the best example of this school. The characters are essentially represented in a Greek iconography: they are naked or dressed in light tunics, the proportions of their bodies are classical. However, the Greek queen Alopé, placed between two talking shepherds, reminds us more or less the goddess of the Kushans Ordokhcho. The hairstyles and costumes of certain characters are equally of the Bactrian type.

The art of engraving of Kharezm

The art of engraving of Kharezm, at the time of the early Middle Ages, was also influenced by several tendencies, but less perceptible than in other regions of Central Asia. The oldest objects date from the second half of the 13th century, the most recent ones from the beginning of the 15th century. All vases made in this region have about the same shape: a half-spherical body soldered onto a ring-shaped pedestal. The representations of the medallions are hammered inside; the side in relief being turned towards the outside. The designs reflect a certain number of themes which played an important role in the cult of local mythology, even though certain representations reveal a Hindu influence.

The art of engraving of Sogdian

The Sogdian art of engraving embodies in a brilliant way the specific features of the style of those days and its diverse tendencies; even though it was influenced by several schools, it became independent around the 6th -7th century. This demonstrated itself through a freer attitude towards existing models, by means of an enrichment of decorative themes and a more vivid and dynamic artistic mode of expression. Great diversity distinguishes the shapes of the silver containers and the procedures used for their ornamentation. Thus slender jugs with thin necks and large pear-shaped bodies, semi-spherical bowls, round dishes, small cups, several figures with ring-handles, embellished with chiselled and engraved designs appeared. Supernatural representations of senmourves (half-bird, half-dogs), winged camels, goats with ritual ribbons, have a specific place within the decoration of the Sogdian art of engraving. The monumental and powerful plastic quality of their shapes, the steady and dynamic lines are characteristic of their style. The representation of real animals: deer, lions, ducks, in free and varied poses, is also specific of the Sogdian art of engraving.

'Oftoba' aquamanile. 19th century. Fine Arts Museum of the Uzbekistan Republic. Tashkent.

'Oftoba' aquamanile and 'dastohui'
basin. 19th century.

'Oftoba' aquamanile. 1930. Museum
of Applied Arts of the Uzbekistan
Republic. Tashkent.

The art of engraving of the Northeast

The art of engraving of the regions of northeast Central Asia (Chach, Ferghana, Semiretchie) has somewhat different forms and decorations than the regions of the centre and the southwest. It also reflects a certain mixture of Sogdian and Turkman traditions and the influence of Byzantine art. Typical of this region are: jugs with winged camels; cups and candelabras with hammered or faceted decoration; round dishes embellished with numerous rosettes; ritual vases with engraved adornments. The decoration list essentially amounts to mammals and birds. Mostly deer and roebucks, horses, camels, sometimes also storks or herons.

In the 9th and 10th century, the heritage of the early Middle Ages was revalued because of the Islamization of Mavera-un-nahr. The particularities of local schools and individual style gradually faded to be taken over by the art of engraving in order to turn to good account a new ideology and artistic practice stemming from Arab tradition.

In the middle of the 11th century we meet with new changes as far as the decorative arts of Central Asia are concerned. In the art of engraving new shapes of vessels become widespread; bronze and copper objects: rectangular and round trays, jugs with spherical bodies and with faceted necks, small cylindrical inkpots, mortars, semi-spherical vases and mirrors made of bronze. The decorative technique mostly used was engraving, extremely convenient for the artistic requirements of that time. The representations of supernatural creatures: the sphinx, winged goats, griffins, mermaids, harpies, senmourves and other figures appreciated in former days remained extremely popular with craftsmen of the 11th and 12th century. These engraved representations are inserted into cartouches or medallions which frame the bodies of the tall jugs and the semi-spherical vases.If plant adornments could already be found in the art of engraving of the early Middle Ages, the introduction and the rapid development of geometrical designs (ghirikh) and arabesques compelled recognition from the 13th century onwards. As time went by, inscriptions (generally in kufic) were stylized and gradually became indecipherable to finish as a sort of original writing adornment. All these designs and inscriptions were made on a background consisting of entangled foliage with round or rectangular spots.

Ornamental skull-cap for a woman's hairstyle. 4th – 5th century. Historical Museum of the Kirghiz Republic, Frounze.

131

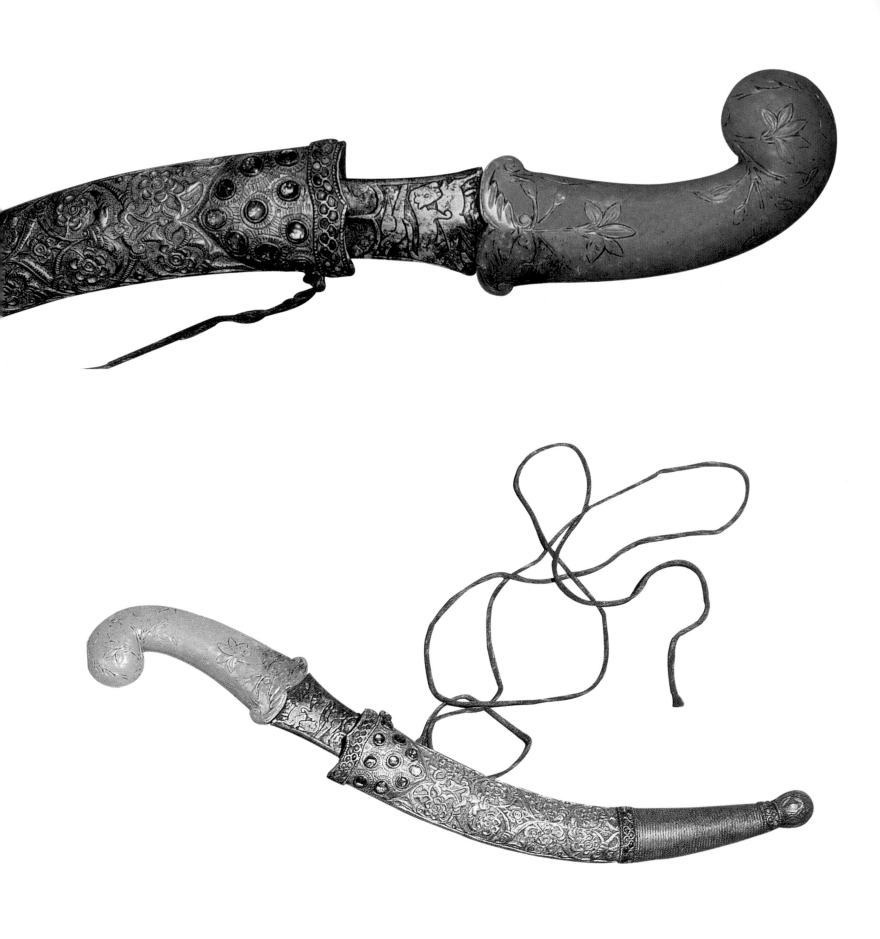

Post-Mongolian times

The period following the Mongolian invasion was marked by an extensive research in decoration, which became even more refined and complex as form became more elegant. The silver wire inlay technique was often used. The artistic traditions of craftsmen of Central Asia in the 14th and 15th century have been revealed to us thanks to works that came from a treasure discovered near Registan in Samarkand, containing over 60 bronze objects for different purposes: cauldrons, vases, bowls, jugs, lids and supports for containers, clearly displaying new tendencies emerging from the art of engraving in Central Asia at that stage of its development. The objects don't all have the same artistic value. The most expressive ones are the small jugs entirely covered with inscriptions of benevolence and figurative subjects carried out with the damascening technique.

It is difficult to form an opinion about the development of the art of engraving in Central Asia throughout the 16th and 17th century although the sources mention the name Usto Kamal, goldsmith of Samarkand, famous for his decorative art on various metal objects.

The museum collections only possess weapon samples of that time. The shields, helmets and sabres embellished with chiseled decoration and precious metal appliqués adorned with semiprecious stones of bright colours, were generally intended for high dignitaries and army commanders.

Many specimens of artistic engraving exist, dating from the 18th - early 19th century. The principal centres of metal object production were Bukhara, Kokand, Khiva, Samarkand, Karchi, Chakhri-Siabz, Tashkent. Although the objects were subject to a common artistic style, with dominating geometrical designs all over, they could be distinguished by numerous particularities.

The works made in Bukhara and Khiva were especially valued. One could recognize them by their gracious forms, well-proportioned classical harmony, stability of ornamental designs mainly made by using the deep engraving technique. The objects made in Samarkand resemble those from Bukhara, because of the way the copper is engraved. In the ornamentation of works from Karchi and Chakhri-Siabz, inlays of turquoise, coral, bright coloured glass and painted backgrounds were used. These objects have shallow engraving and small fragmented designs. The form of the vessels is complex and makes them seem heavy. Stone inlay and shallow engraving was also employed by the craftsmen from Kokand, principal centre of artistic metal work in the Ferghana valley. The shapes of the objects, the ornamentation and the decorative procedures are more developed there than in Karchi and Chakhri-Siabz.

Dagger. 19th century. Detail. Museum of the History of the Peoples of Uzbekistan. Tashkent.

Dagger. 19th century. Khiva, Museum of the History of the Peoples of Uzbekistan. Tashkent.

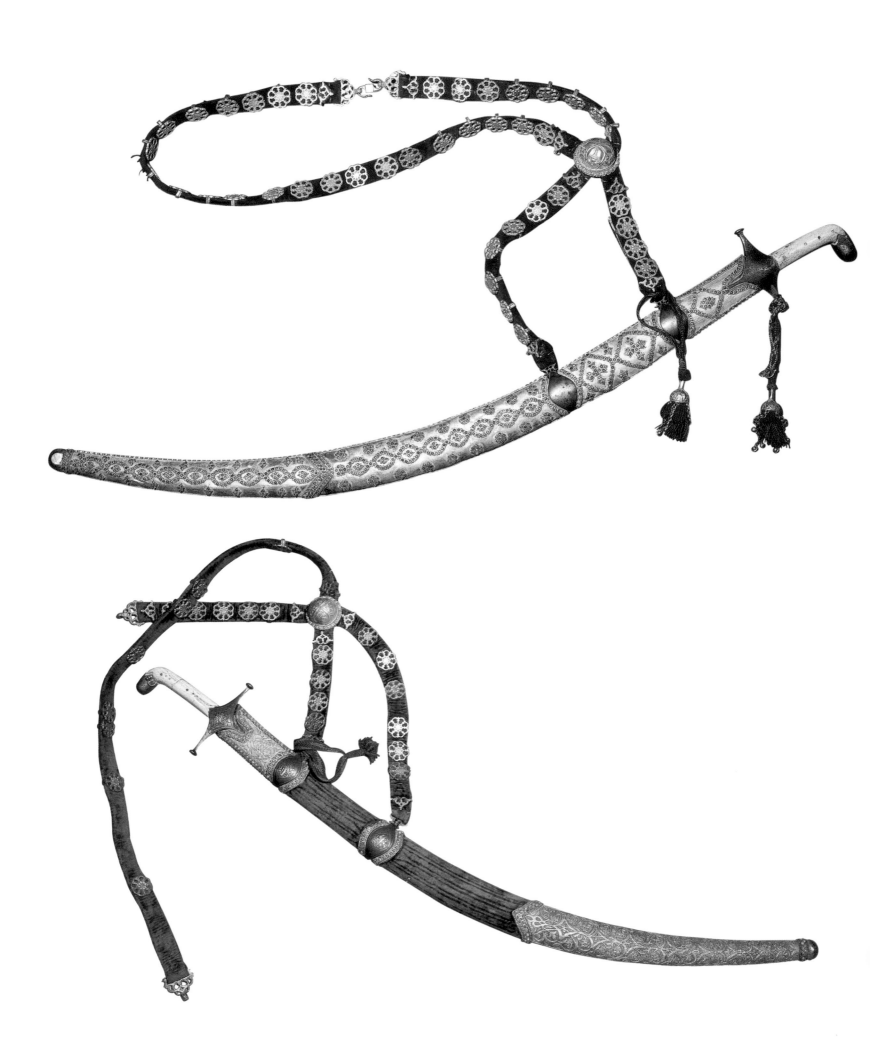

The contemporary period

At the end of the 19th - early 20th century, reproductions of architectural monuments and supernatural monsters inspired by very popular lithographic works in those days, appeared in the engraved decoration of Ferghana and Bukhara. The objects of this period had different shapes and purposes.

The crockery of engraved copper was the same in each centre. It was composed of elegant jugs, washbowls, teapots, with round, slightly flattened bodies, round and rectangular plates, vases and container with handles for water, milk and other drinks, candelabra, censers, perfume flasks, etc. The technical ornamentation procedures were almost identical everywhere. Essentially they consisted of craving, engraving and hemstitched decoration. The vessels of big dimensions (buckets, cauldrons) sometimes had simple ornamentation. Very often richly embellished metalware was used for decorative purposes in the houses of the well-to-do citizens.

The Goldsmith's trade

The art of the goldsmith in Central Asia reflects many aspects of the material and spiritual life of its people, their way of life, their religious, social, ethical and artistic aspirations.

Antiquity and the Middle Ages

The Bactrian goldsmith-jewellers excelled in the art of embedding turquoises and almandites and knew how to treat and shape metal in different ways: casting, engraving, filigreeing, milling. The jewels of antiquity reflect the style, common in art, which goes back to the traditions of Persia, Greece, India and the Oriental steppes. After close observation of the sculptures and wall-paintings of palaces and temples in Central Asia, one can appreciate the jewellery of the end of antiquity and the beginning of the Middle Ages (3rd - 8th century): necklaces, bracelets, belt-buckles, rings and earrings. Besides gold jewellery, useful objects were made out of copper and bronze throughout this period: brooches, amulets, clothing elements, belts adorned with representations of human beings, birds and animals.

The art of the goldsmith in the 9th - 13th century undergoes the same style changes as the other crafts. The pieces of work are provided with Arab inscriptions framing zoomorphic subjects included in round medallions, made either in relief or with openwork.

Swords. 19th century.

The clothing elements cast in silver, bronze and copper are quite predominant: brooches, belt trimmings, ornamental plaques, amulets and fasteners representing animals. The chronicles and poetic works of this period contain many descriptions of this jewellery and luxury goods made of gold and silver with an astonishing abundance of gems adorning them: diamonds, rubies, emeralds, turquoises, pearls. These stones will still be valued in the jewellery of the following centuries (14th - 16th century), as the search for a certain refinement of shape, decoration and techniques of jewellery leads to more and more diversity.

Modern times

The miniatures of the 16th and 17th century show us jewellery of which the style will be perpetuated until the beginning of the 20th century.

The art of the goldsmith of this last period is apparent in all its ethnographic multiplicity, with great diversity of shape, material, technical procedures and types of objects. One can appreciate the craft of the goldsmiths by observing the sheaths of sabres, the hilts of daggers with refined filigree patterns, the plates of harnesses and gilded silver adorning the belts with embedded precious stones. But the goldsmiths of those days were essentially occupied with jewellery for women. All the events in the life of women of Central Asia, from their youth until old age, are reflected in the nature and quality of the jewellery they possessed. Some of them were wedding presents and were worn only during feastdays, quite different from what one would wear every day; but other gradations also existed and were linked with social status, age, etc. Parents gave their daughter, aged from three to seven years old, silver earrings and bracelets, coral jewellery of little value. On the other hand, jewellery given to a fiancée showed great diversity. Mothers passed on family jewels to their daughter, but usually the fiancé ordered engagement jewellery from a goldsmith, and offered it to his future wife throughout his first visits. This jewellery formed a rich unity, harmoniously completing the ample dresses with bright colours magnificently embroidered by skilled hands. The jewellery adorned the head, the forehead, the temples, the ears, the plaits, the neck, chest, shoulders, wrists and fingers. During wedding and feast days, girls and young women would wear all the jewellery in their possession.

Mask. 4th – 5th century. Tchou Valley, Kirghizie. Historical Museum of the Kirghiz Republic, Frounze.

The large-sized jewellery was generally made of silver (sometimes of gilded silver); the earrings, rings and bracelets however were made of gold. The goldsmiths used almost every known procedure for the shaping of the metal: forging, casting, stamping, engraving, chasing, filigreeing. Moreover, the objects were adorned with gilt and niello, and coloured stones were embedded in them. The goldsmiths from Uzbekistan (zargar) and Tadjikistan generously adorned their pieces of work with semiprecious stones. The pieces of lesser value were embellished with glass jewellery, sequins and coral.

Schools of the goldsmith's trade

In the 19th century several schools of the goldsmith's trade opened in Uzbekistan and Tadjikistan: Bukhara, Samarkand, Chakhri-Siabz, Khiva, Tashkent, Kokand, Khodjent, Marghilan, Oura-Tubé and Ach were the main centres. These schools were specialized in the manufacturing of jewellery. The tiara of gilded silver adorned with turquoises and gems, represented the principal piece of women's jewellery. The tiara was made from a plate in the shape of an arc of a circle decorated with symmetrical openwork composed of a network of intertwined shanks on which stones and pearls were set; it was worn with temporal inlaid with polychrome stones. At late 19th - early 20th century, a profusion of embedded stones, a complexity of lines and a certain eclecticism of style, can be noticed in the goldsmith trade. In Turkestan this coincides with the appearance of Russian and Tartarian pieces of jewellery, which the local craftsmen imitated to satisfy the taste of a rich clientele.

'Kamar' man's belt. 19th century.
Fine Arts Museum of the Uzbekistan Republic. Tashkent.

'Bibichak' pendants. 19th century.

Women's jewellery

The women of the south of Tadjikistan and Uzbekistan adorned their foreheads with little disks of stamped silver strung in several rows. In these regions it was also the custom to wear little silver spherical bells suspended from cords, and strips of cloth covered with silver plates were used for the adornment of hair. In Bukhara metal brooches were in vogue, with the tip shaped like a flat medallion or stylized bird.

In Kharezm, the headress of young girls was crowned with a kind of silver faceted skullcap, adorned with coloured stones or glass. Splendid polychrome pectorals were worn exclusively by rich women. Another more common ornament was a big medallion fastened with several rows of small chains. It was more austere in style.

Necklaces of coral beads combined with plaques or coins were very much in vogue in the mountainous regions of Tadjikistan and in the south of Uzbekistan. The goldsmiths took great care of the manufacturing of brooches closing the upper part of women's clothes.

The openwork silver medallion-shaped fastenings, embellished on the sides with pendants and reminding us of the solar disk, were very popular in the south of Tadjikistan.

In Central Asia, amulets were very much in vogue. One or two of them were usually worn on the chest, or around the forearms. They had different names and shapes, but the manufacturing technique was the same. Generally they would be presented as small silver boxes, in which women would enclose extracts of the Koran.

The sacred nature of this ornament lost its influence at the end of the 19th century and became a simple piece of jewellery finely worked. The remarkable delicacy of necklaces embellished with plates and leaf-shaped pendants, the high mastery of ornamental gilt and the embedded cornaline, class this ornament amongst the most admirable pieces of work of the decorative arts of the peoples of Central Asia.

'Kultyk-Tumor' amulet-holder. 19th century. Fine Arts Museum of the Uzbekistan Republic. Tashkent.

Sarsouzan hair ornament. End of the 19th century – beginning of the 20th century. Boukhara. Fine Arts Museum of the Uzbekistan Republic. Tashkent.

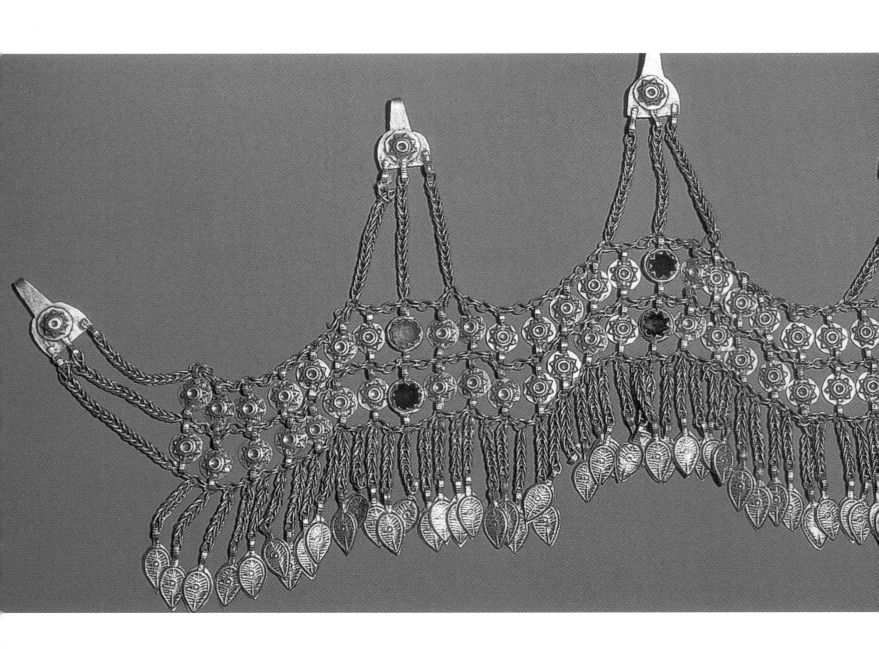

'Sinssila' frontal hair ornament. 19th century. Museum of Archaeology, History and the Fine Arts. Dusanbe.

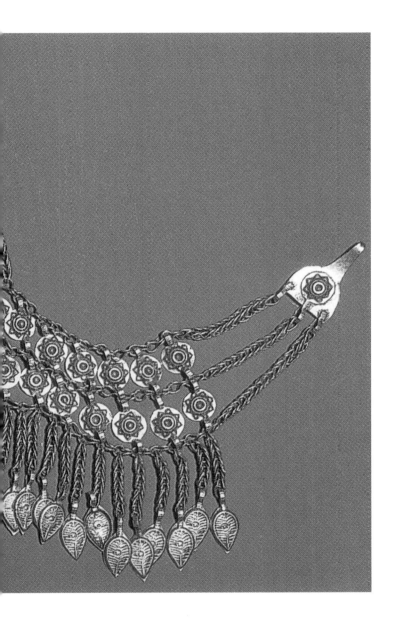

Gold Jewelry. National Museum of
Georgia. Tbilissi.

'Kochtillo' frontal hair ornament.
1920. Museum of Archaeology, History
and the Fine Arts. Dusanbe.

Hair helmet worn by the women of
Karakapakstan.

Earrings adorned with milling, embellished with filigreed or stamped openwork designs, inlaying and pearl pendants, turquoises or corals, are distinguished by their great diversity. Each town, each region, possessed its favourite models of earrings. In terms of bracelets, there were two types which are still popular even today: open, or a closed circle. Generally they were made of silver, more rarely made of gold, brass, copper, bronze or made of pearls. The metal bracelets were embellished with stamped designs, niello or engraved, set with turquoises or coloured glass. Sometimes the exterior surface of the bracelets was adorned with significance at a particular period.

Pendants. 1930s. North Tadjikistan.
Museum of Archaeology, History and
the Fine Arts. Dusanbe.

Earrings. 1920 – 1930. Sourkhan-Daria
region. Fine Arts Museum of the
Uzbekistan Republic. Tashkent.

Female hairstyle from the Taxkurgan
region.

Necklace (Rokhti-mougra). End of the 19th century. Kouliab, Museum of Archaeology, History and the Fine Arts. Dusanbe.

'Soeko' breast plate. 1910. Fine Arts Museum of the Kirghiz Republic. Frunze.

'Guliaka' buckle. 20th century. Fine Arts Museum of the Turkmenistan Republic. Achkhabad.

The Craft industry

At different times in Central Asia, besides metal, stone and terracotta ware, a number of objects were fashioned from other materials: glass, ivory, leather, wood. The skill shown by craftsmen also manifested itself in felt-working, carpet weaving, cloth printing and embroidery.

Glass

Some specimens of unique glass objects dating from the early Middle Ages have come down to us, but glass making was to flourish during the 9th - 13th century. It was in those days that glassware, chemical implements, perfume flasks, etc. became widespread. Figurative designs were rare and always produced by engraving or the glass-blowing mould technique. The glass objects in the shape of figurines and the medallions with engraved ornaments in relief from the palaces of Aphrasiab and Termez are of great originality. They are adorned with plant designs, horses and riders, birds, fishes, various animals, hunting scenes, wildcats; sometimes they are covered with epigraphic ornamentation.

Ivory work

In Central Asia ivory work already existed in ancient times. Alongside usual utensils made of bone, in antiquity there were true masterpieces of ivory: plaques engraved with religious and profane subjects, chess pieces of Dalverzine-tépé, as well as a great number of admirable rhytons discovered in the palace of the Parthian monarch at Staraïa-Nissa. These objects reveal great diversity of local artistic traditions, Siberian-Altaic, Hindu-Buddhist, Persian and Hellenistic. Many of them have maintained a considerable purity of style, but sometimes various artistic movements mingle, creating new kinds of heterogeneous works. In the Middle Ages (5th - 16th century) practical objects predominated considerably (earpicks, plates, etc.), although some pieces of work of real artistic value reached us. For instance the pieces of a chess-set from Samarkand in the 11th and 12th century.

Between the 17th and the 19th centuries, ivory was used for the decoration of pommels, sheaths, rifle butts. National musical instruments, made of precious wood, were inlaid with small ivory plaques as they are today.

Chess pieces. 12th century.
Historical Museum of the Art and
Culture of the Uzbekistan Republic.
Samarkand.

Containers of molten glass. 11th –
12th century. Aphrasiab, History
Museum of Samarkand.

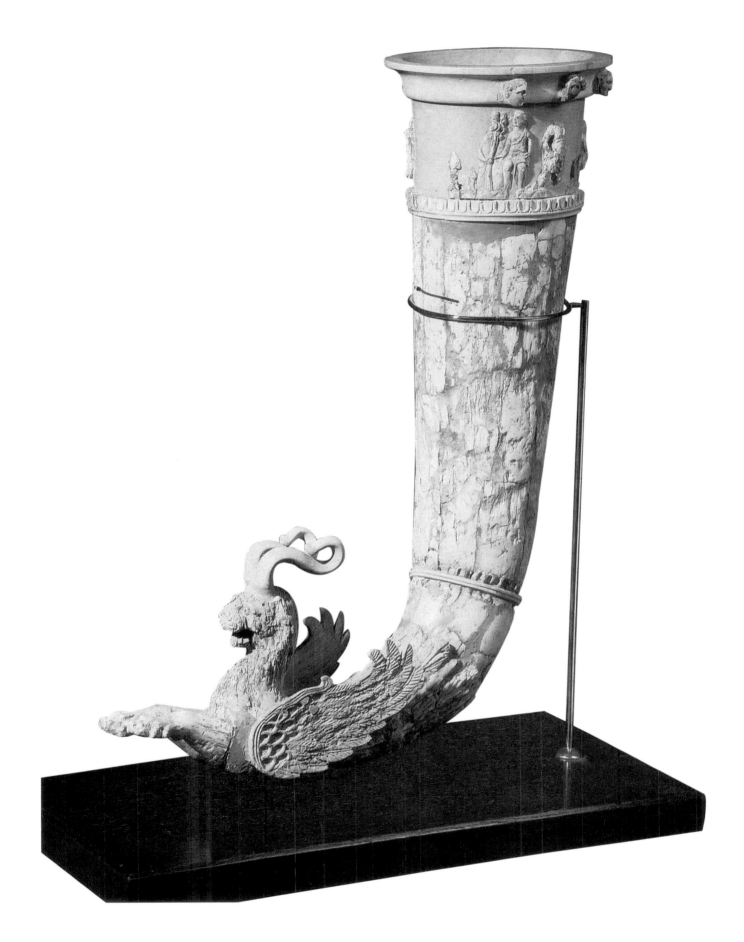

Rhyton. 2nd – 1st century B.C.
Historical Museum of the
Turkmenistan Republic.

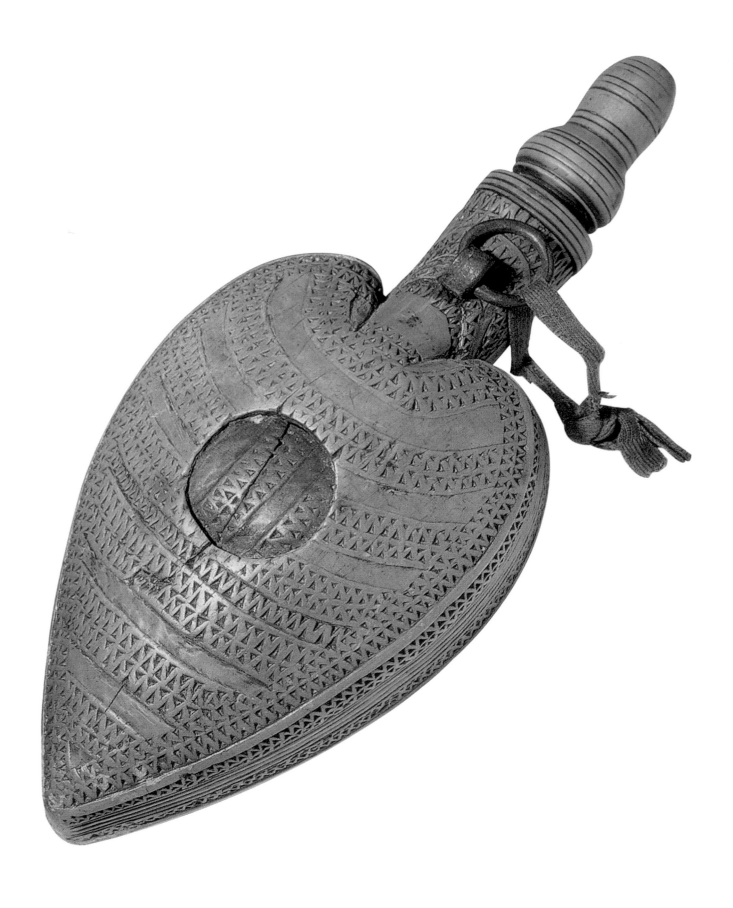

'Obdon' water gourde. 19th – 20th
century. Museum of Archeology,
History and the Fine Arts. Dusanbe.

Woodcarving and painted wood

Numerous architectural monuments of the early and late Middle Ages witness the rich and ancient traditions of woodcutting. The woodcutters who worked on the architectural interiors would simultaneously produce practical objects. The wood of linen chests, cradles, cupboards, bookstands, caskets, low tables, was adorned with carved designs. The wooden musical instruments were also richly decorated. In the second half of the 19th century many decorative polyhedral tables and stools appeared for the European population living in the towns of Central Asia. In the late 19th - early 20th century, woodcutting schools opened in Khiva, Bukhara, Samarkand, Kokand, and Khodjent. Even today they still have a good reputation. In order to decorate practical wooden objects, the craftsmen used two methods: simple hollow ornamentation technique or woodcutting called "bottomless".

Book-holder. 19th – 20th century. Museum of Archaeology, History and the Fine Arts. Dusanbe.

156

In the mountainous regions of Tadjikistan, Kirghizstan, Karakalpakie, woodcutters refined the decoration of clogs, crockery, chests, and other wooden objects. The decoration of these pieces of work were composed of designs with triangles, hooks and other geometrical elements, creating simple adornment, devoid of artifice and sometimes archaic. The aim was to turn to good account the natural beauty of wood. The technique of "bottomless" woodcutting was only used by professional woodcutters. It was a highly developed urban craft. The basis of these ornaments consisted of islimis, the supple and dynamic entanglement of foliage strewn with buds, flowers and leaves, and with pargori, austere and static geometrical designs traced with a pair of compasses and a ruler.

The painting of wood, like woodcutting used for interior decoration since remote times, was also used for the adornment of practical objects. Complex floral and geometrical designs were applied on the finished surface of small tables, chests, small boxes, turntables and other objects. Then the design was painted with a very thin brush, using mineral or plant colours embellished with bronze or silver. Favourite colours were red, green and blue.

Table. 1954. Fine Arts Museum of the Uzbekistan Republic. Tashkent.

'Tchang' zither. 1940.

'Egar' saddle. 1930.

The Potters, panel. 1977. Museum of
Archaeology, History and the Fine Arts.
Dusanbe.

Felt-working

From ancient times, felt was an irreplaceable material in the life of the nomads of Central Asia. The material did not require any specific working technique and was profoundly anchored in the culture. In the 19th century, the manufacturing of felt (*kochma*) was particularly widespread among the Kirghizans and Turkmans. The material was covered with decorations or indented and appliqué patterns, sometimes adorned with embroidery. The work with applied decoration was exclusively done by the Kirghizans and the Kazakhans.

Two techniques existed: one called "filled decoration", the other one "appliqué decoration". The first technique consisted of long and laborious work: coarse wool was arranged on a mat which represented the background; on top of this, the ornamental design would be traced by using wool tufts of various colours. After moistening, it was rolled up and filled. This way, the first layer and the ornament stuck together closely.

Previous page:
Yurt, traditional Kirghiz tent. Historical Museum of the Kirghiz Republic.

'Asmaldyk' camel armor. 18th century. Ethnographic Museum. St Petersburg.

'Ensi' Door Covering. 19th century. Russian Museum. St Petersburg.

163.

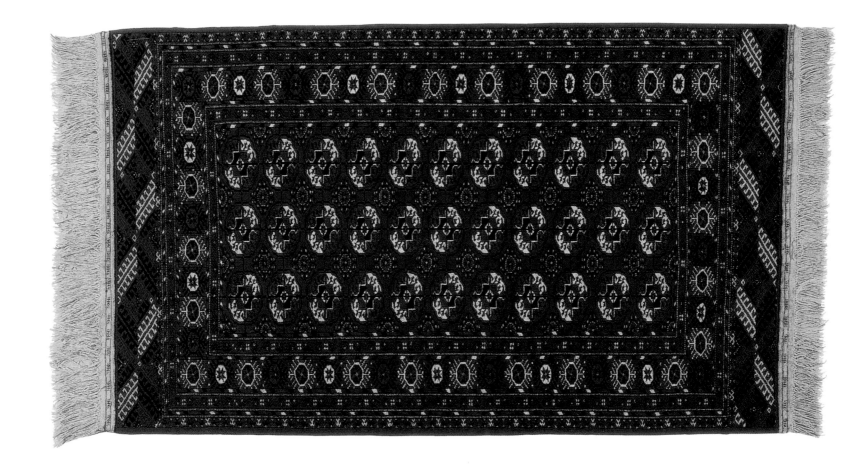

'Khaly' floor carpet. 1970.
Ethnographic Museum. St Petersburg.

The kochma were normally rectangular with a dark brown background and an ornament made of big medallions. Concerning felt from Turkmenistan, vivid red shades and bright yellow predominated over green and blue. Concerning Kirghizan felt, pink, orange and raspberry shades were added. The patterns graciously mingled with the background through the progressive gradation of colour. The essential ornamentation element of felt is a horned design well known among breeders. Considering felt works with indented decoration, one has to mention the strips which adorned the inside of the yurts' domes, various bags intended for storing of clothes, cups, dishes, wooden spoons and other utensils. Great care was taken of these pieces of work, because they ended up in the bride's trousseau and could rarely be bought.

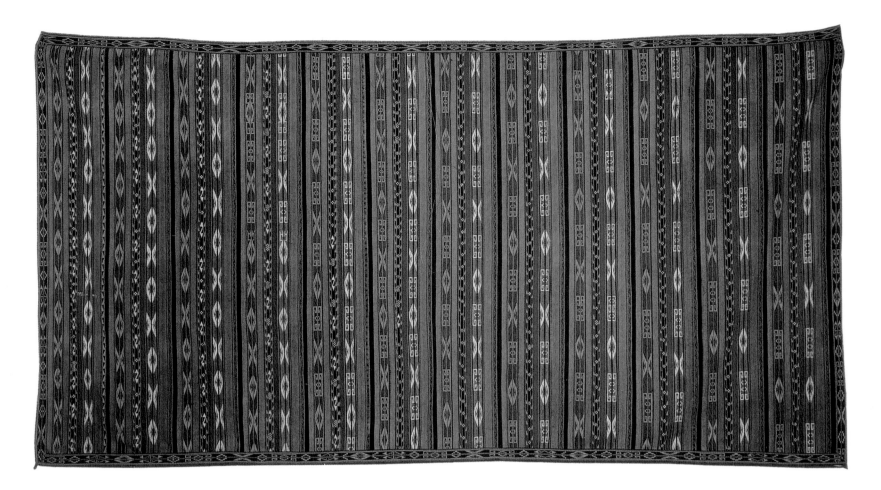

The felt with "appliqué decoration", embroidered and trimmed with fringes, was mainly used to warm the yurt. In order to decorate the felt works, the Kirghizan women were masters at the appliqué technique and did not only use felt for this, but also leather, velvet, woollen cloth and other fabrics. The yurt's frame was adorned with scarlet felt; on the white felt of the door, red and blue ornaments were stitched.

Utilitarian objects of small dimensions were embellished with appliqués consisting of other materials.

Nowadays, small felt pieces are sold as souvenirs and the kochma, because of their high decorative value, are very much in vogue and decorate the houses of the urban and rural population.

'Bechkete' carpet. 1960-1970. Fine Arts Museum of the Kirghiz Republic. Frunze.

'Paliate' mural embroidery.
19th – 20th century. Fine Arts
Museum of the Uzbekistan Republic.
Tashkent.

'Khaly' floor carpet. 19th century.
Russian Museum. St Petersburg.

Carpet weaving

The production of woven carpets is one of the most laborious crafts. Archaeologists have discovered samples of woven carpets dating from the first centuries B.C. Writers of ancient Greece, Rome, the Arab world and Persia, mention that the weaving of carpets flourished in Central Asia ever since the 2nd century B.C. We can still imagine what the carpets of Central Asia were like, by looking at the monumental paintings of the early Middle Ages and the Oriental miniatures of more recent periods.

Numerous museums and private collections preserve the carpets of Central Asia of the 19th and early 20th century. In those days almost all the tribes of the region produced woven carpets with a short pile. The knot-stitched carpets were mainly produced by the Turkmans, and partly by the Kirghizan and the Uzbekan breeder tribes. The carpets of Central Asia, with short and long pile, had different purposes: floor coverings, prayer mats (djaïnamaz), yurt portieres were widespread. The woven practical objects were exceptional for their expressiveness and finishing. Oblong bags suspended with straps from the yurt's frame in which clothes or crockery and food were put away. Various types of carpets were used for the harnessing of horses: saddle cloths, covers, saddlebow-bags (khourdjines), generally made with woven cloth and adorned with decorative strips.

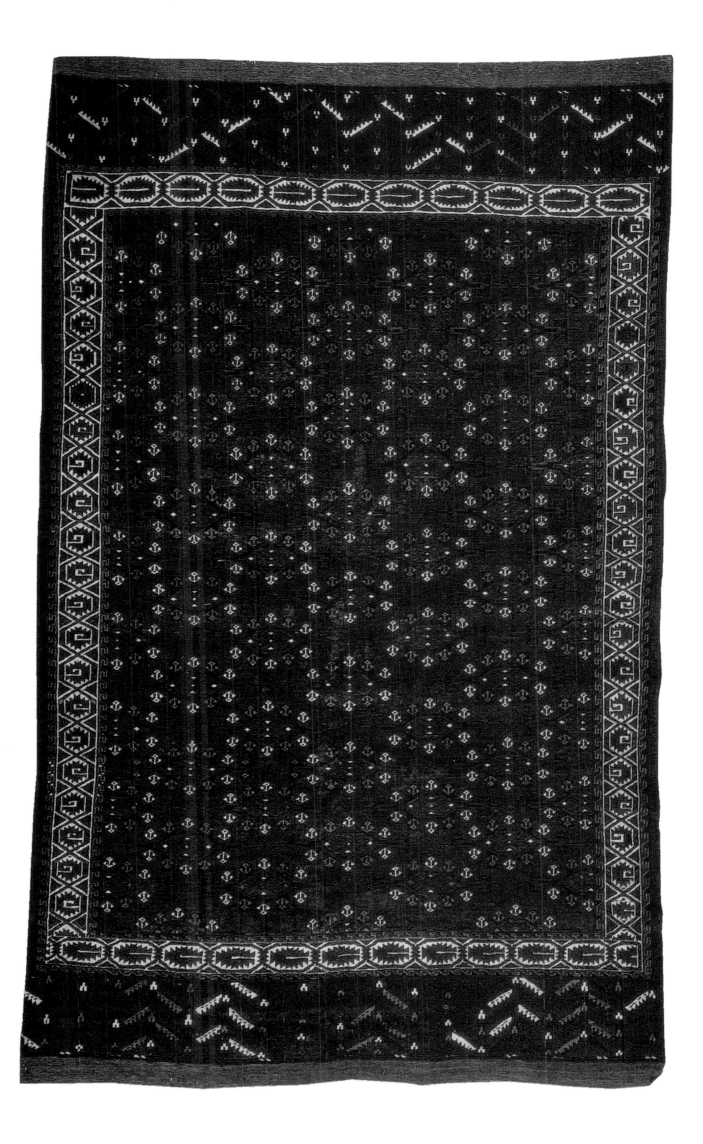

The Turkmans were very attentive to the decoration of carpets covering the camels leading a wedding procession. On one of these camels the bride was led to her husband's house. For important events, the Kirghizans covered their camels with long carpets reaching the ground, and young camels had smaller carpets woven especially for them, according to their height.

The quality of wool, colouring, dyeing methods and weaving techniques were very much taken into account in carpetmaking. The weavers preferred wool which was long, light-coloured, soft, strong, shorn in spring, slightly wavy, possessing a certain brilliance. These conditions were essential to obtain a supple yarn of high quality; easy to dye, resistant and practical for the weaving loom, assuring well-made carpets. Camel and goat wool was used for the weaving of household objects.

Until 1870, colouring extracted from plants, for stable and saturated colours, was used. Since the end of the 19th century, the use of aniline-based colouring, for cheaper and brighter colours, has negatively affected the quality of carpets. The noble range of cherry shades and red-ochre of the ancient carpets is replaced by more vivid and gaudy colours, quickly losing their original aspect because of the bad quality of colouring.

The carpets of Central Asia were woven on very elementary horizontal looms of two different types: narrow and broad. The archaic style of the looms contrasts with the astonishing beauty and quality of the carpets woven on them. On the narrow looms, which can be easily dismantled, rugs were woven for the yurts, and narrow strips stitched together formed floor coverings. The broad looms, which were long used (not in the yards but in the houses or the yurts), were used for weaving big carpets with knot-stitches.

The surface of the carpets consisted of the entanglement of the weft threads with the warp threads. Velvet was obtained by the knotting of wool strands of various colours. These strands were knotted by hand, according to a chosen knot. Then the ends were cut to obtain velvet. According to the technique used, two groups of rugs can be distinguished. The first one includes the carpets usually woven throughout Central Asia, with the decoration obtained by the entanglement of the coloured weft threads with the warp threads: these were the ground and passage sheets, shoulder bags (khourdjine) and other bags (tchouval, torba), which were remarkable for their refined graphic designs and intensity of colour.

Tapestry (Chirdak). 1960s-70s. Tchou Valley, Kirghiz. Historical Museum of the Kirghiz Republic, Frounze.

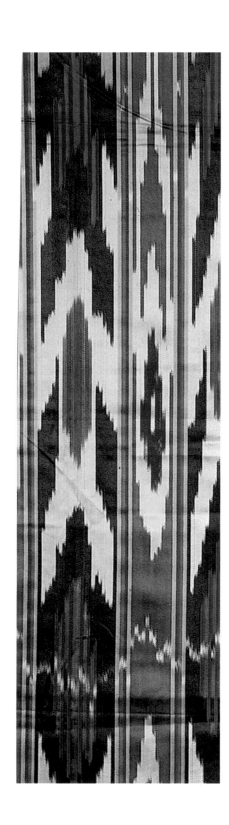

The second group includes carpets of which the decoration is formed by the coloured warp threads covering the weft threads on both sides.

They were used as groundsheets or for making bedspreads, various bags, hangings to adorn the place where the young bride slept during the first days of her marriage.

Throughout the centuries, numerous generations of weavers established common principles of decorative composition and colour combinations for all the schools of the region. The central part of the carpet, usually demarcated by a narrow selvage, enclosed the principal designs of the ornamentation, which was repeated to form vertical and horizontal rows according to a principle of symmetry on two axes.

With carpets of smaller dimensions, the decoration fitted into the central medallion. The harmonious fusion of decoration and background was created by the judicious choice of the range of colour. Normally the background was made in red shades and the decoration was cream-coloured or dark brown, more rarely dark blue or green. Sometimes the weavers (generally Turkomans) introduced the same shades in the decoration as in the background; this would add a particular harmony to the piece of work. The carpet's colour was distributed in squares and diagonals. A well-balanced static composition was created by the first technique, which was more typical of the Kirghizan carpets.

With the diagonal harmonization of the colour of decorative elements, a practice adopted by the Turkmans, the overall decor of carpets acquired a dynamic character and an especially expressive rhythm.

A well-defined unity of ornamental subjects evolved in Central Asia, including stylized zoomorphic and plant designs, signs, of cosmogony and heraldry, symbolical representations of objects endowed with protective powers, various geometrical figures. Every type of carpet, according to its purpose, had its own specific patterns, following the traditional composition of carpets of the 19th - early 20th century.

Fabric Samples. 1960s-70s. Marguilan. Museum of the Applied Arts of the Uzbekistan Republic.

Printed cloth

For millennia, various types of printed cloth have been produced in Central Asia. Multicoloured silk was used for making clothes, curtains, and other items. In the 7th - 8th century, Sogdian silk called zandanatchi (after the name of the town Zandana, near Bukhara) was already famous. The designs enclosed in the medallions surrounded with pearls represented supernatural animals (winged animals with four legs) and real ones (elephants, goats, birds), plant patterns, mythological scenes, religious cults. The making of cloth continued throughout the 9th and 10th century with a mixture of cotton. In those days the principal centres of cloth production were Merv, Bukhara and Samarkand. Weaving attained its apogee between the 14th and the 16th century in the kingdom of the Timurides. The written sources tell us so, and so do the cloth models one can examine in the miniatures.

In the 17th and the 18th century, plain and illustrated zandanatchis were made of cotton, wool, silk and mixed silk, and also of cotton cloth, velvet and satin. The production of silk and half-silk cloth represents an originality in Asian weaving of the 19th - early 20th century. With this type of cloth the weft thread determined the decoration; that's why it was slightly displaced on the loom, causing blurred lines and the forming of designs recalling the outlines of clouds. Printing cloth by means of a stencil was traditional. Stencils were used for making dresses, shawls, but also tablecloths, curtains, and blankets. Bukhara was the indisputable centre of this craft, but the cloths of Samarkand, Ferghana, Khodjent, Tashkent were also very much appreciated. In the 19th - early 20th century, printed cloth still existed in various colours. But from then on, only red and black designs were printed on cloth. For the manufacturing of printed cloth they just used cotton cloth, soaked in a special liquid on which the design was transferred with the help of engraved plates. The designs were abstract or represented bushes with dense foliage, gracious buds, entangled branches with leaves, pomegranates, and almonds alternating in a rhythmical way.

'Rui-djo' nuptial bedcover. 1916.
Museum of Archeology, History and
the Fine Arts. Dusanbe.

Festival tunic. 1905-1907.

Gandora. 1900-1904. Fine Arts Museum of the Uzbekistan Republic. Tashkent.

Embroidery

Almost all tribes of Central Asia embellished their clothes and practical objects with embroidery. There were many resemblances between Tadjikan and Uzbekan embroidery. This art was so widespread that today still, in many rural regions of Tadjikistan and Uzbekistan, the walls of rooms are adorned with embroidered strips, reminding us of friezes and decorated panels; bedspreads, wedding sheets, little bags to preserve tea, mirror covers, dresses for women and children, belts for men, skullcaps (tioubétéiki) are embellished with embroidery. Plant patterns are the essential designs, and rosettes frequently occur in the decoration of mural panels.

Until the end of the 19th century, silk thread and wool were used for embroidering on white or cream-coloured cotton cloth, woven on a loom with handles. The appearance of industrial cloth with colours and various threads tinted with artificial dyes made the embroidery lose its quality; the designs became many-coloured and the colours were no longer fast.

Each region or centre possessed its proper designs and colours; contrasting colours and ornaments of big dimensions characterized the goods from Samarkand and Oura-Tubé. The design of the panels from Bukhara, Ferghana and Tashkent, very lyrical in tone, could be recognized by a great diversity of raspberry shades, pale green and purple.

'Pechonaband' frontal headband.
20th century. Fine Arts Museum of the Uzbekistan Republic. Tashkent.

Reversable Chapan Robe. C. 1870.
Hand-woven. Boukhara, Uzbekistan.

Trousers. 1910. Fine Arts Museum of the Kirghiz Republic. Frunze.

Skirt (beldemetchi). 1926. Kirghiz. Fine Arts Museum of the Kirghiz Republic. Frunze.

'Chadar'. 1930. Fine Arts Museum of the Turkmenistan Republic. Achkhabad.

Golden embroidery, a particularity of the embroidery of Central Asia, flourished towards the middle of the 19th century in Bukhara. It was a craft reserved for men and was passed on from father to son; the embroidery was done with golden and "silver thread and was used for gandouras", belts, trousers, the shoes of emirs and noble people at court. The rich caparisons of the horses and the shabracks were also adorned with golden embroidery, as well as household objects like pillowcases, bedspreads, wallets, knife cases, etc. Golden embroidery was done on velvet of dark shades: purple, blue, green. The decorative designs of golden embroidery were mostly plant-like; zoomorphic and geometrical designs were rarely encountered.

Embroidery was also used for the different felt elements of the yurt, the hangings, passages, storage bags, household utensils, objects for harnessing horses. The Kirghizan embroideresses knew a great variety of stitches. Patterns of stylized leaves, bushes, flowers predominated in their deigns, and more rarely geometrical and zoomorphic patterns.

Traditional Turkman embroidery was essentially used for the decoration of national costumes. Until about the end of the 19th century, they were cut out of woollen or silk cloth made by craftsmen. But from the 20th century on, only cloth produced by industry was used and coloured blue, green, yellow, and above all red, the favourite colour which symbolized life, youth and nature's invigorating strengths. A specific stitch and an original design corresponded with each detail of the clothing. Plant-like volutes, flower buds, tulips, symbols of fertility, predominated in the designs. Representations of teapots, vases, jewellery, stylized animal figures with protective powers and benevolent symbols were sometimes embroidered.

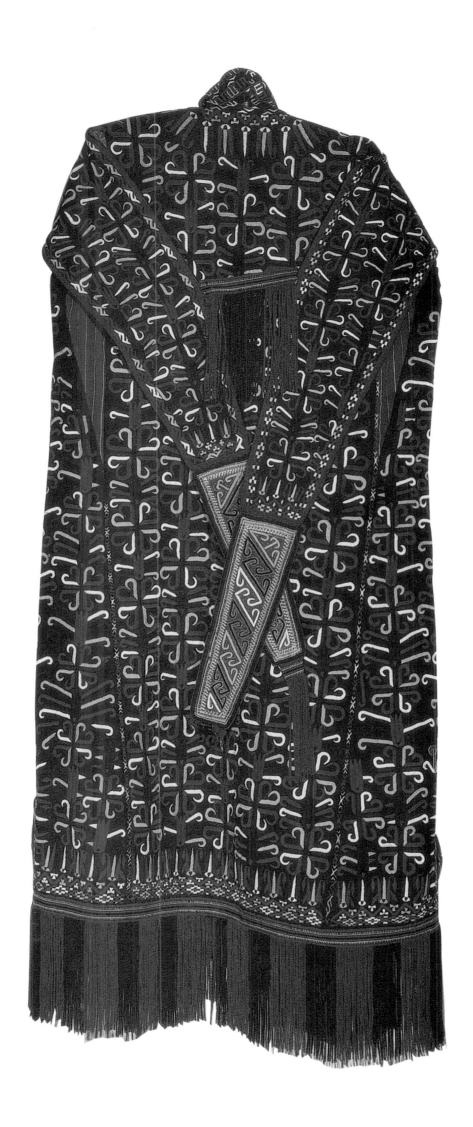

Tunic. 1979. Museum of Archeology,
History and the Fine Arts. Dusanbe.

Young Turkish girls in traditional dress.

'Tissa-koptchik' purse and 'tchyny-kap' wallet . 19th – 20th century. Fine Arts Museum of the Uzbekistan Republic. Tashkent.

Leatherwork

Leather goods had a particular place amongst the traditional practical objects of the tribes of Central Asia in the 18th - early 19th century. The raw material was the skin of various animals, used for pale green shagreen, tanned youfte (Russian leather), morocco and suede. Rich procedures for the ornamentation of objects had been elaborated: stamping, embroidery, the use of tanned leather or silver plates adorned with niello.

The artistic working of leather was not only well known to nomads, but also in the big towns of Central Asia. In the noisy marketplaces of Bukhara and Samarkand, expert craftsmen embroidered suede hunting-trousers, fur boots, cushions, wallets, belts for men, while the client watched. Horse harnesses were carefully adorned. The covers and the leather harness were adorned with silver plates, little spherical bells embellished with niello, cornaline and turquoise inlays. The stamped ornaments of bookcovers and paper-files used by scientists and theologians were elegantly refined. Yet one can observe an excessive ornamentation of leather objects from the end of the 19th - beginning of the 20th century.

Traditional forms and a pureness of style were characteristic of the leather objects made by the Kirghizans, the Kazakhans and the Karakalpakans, who had lived a uniquely nomadic life in the past. Besides clothes and the horse's harness which were made of leather, crockery for the preservation of koumys (fermented mare's milk) was also made of leather. After having been treated, the hides were tanned and sewn. The container thus obtained was filled with earth or sand, and on the damp surface of the hide a decoration was drawn with a sharp stick. When the form and the designs had dried, the earth was removed and the object smoked for several days in smokehouses especially constructed for this purpose. The form was then filled with water to clean it from the smoke and soot.

The stamping technique was also applied by using carved wooden moulds. The moist leather was pushed against the carved wood and the ornament appeared in relief.

Various kinds of leather containers exist. The most original ones, considering their shape and decoration, were tumblers (kookor), of which the contours remind us of the curved horns of the ibex. Often they were decorated with voluted, circular or triangular ornaments with representations of stylized birds and animals honoured by tribes of breeders. By using several layers of leather, cylindrical cases were manufactured in which cups, fitted into each other, could be put away.

There were semi-spherical cases as well, with contours resembling an inverted cup. They were embellished with a stamped or engraved design, silver strips and plates decorated with niello. The design of the leather containers was disposed according to their shape. Patterns linked with ancient magical representations were used in the ornamentation. Numerous elements recall the designs of carpets, embroideries, and Kirghizan jewellery.

The frequent travels due to nomadic life made these leather containers practical and they became, thanks to the talent of the craftsmen, marvellous samples of artistic works.

A general picture of popular crafts

Just as modern artists, painters, graphic artists, sculptors, refer to the past in their creative work, craftsmen are sustained by the thousand-year-old traditions of their people, in spite of the radical changes which followed the establishment of the Soviet regime, the development of creative cartels and commercial networks for selling. Nowadays, the popular decorative arts in the republics of Central Asia have developed in different ways. Numerous craftsmen work at home again, obtaining raw materials and selling their articles individually at traditional markets on Sundays. Generally they are craftsmen specialized in embroidery, the manufacturing of felt and woollen carpets, who live in rural communities. Now, traditional crafts are incorporated into the industry of art objects. Many popular masters work within companies of the ministries of light industry: manufacturers of porcelain, carpet factories, embroidery workshops and workshops producing souvenir articles.

At the time of the establishment of the Soviet regime, many regional nomadic tribes had ceased to move about. This brought about radical changes in their lifestyle and artistic awareness. Many utilitarian objects of the past have become souvenirs. And yet today the native population still widely uses traditional products of the decorative arts in everyday life. In the same way modern popular ceramics largely perpetuate the tradition of the schools established in the 19th century.

Front dress-piece for a horse (gozluk). End of the 19th century. Historic Museum of the Turkistan Republic, Achkhabad.

Decorative style and technical particularities allow us to distinguish three main centres: the school of the Northeast with Ferghana, the school of the centre with Bukhara and Samarkand, and the school of the Southwest with Kharezm, including certain regions of Uzbekistan and Turkmenistan.

Nowadays, the ceramics of the northwestern and eastern regions of Central Asia are the most diversified, in the form and content of their decorative designs. They include medium and big sized vases, large dishes, jugs, containers of different shapes for dairy products, bowls, pitchers, etc. The ornament of the crockery created by these craftsmen is more refined and smaller than that of the artists from Kharezm and gives an impression of lyricism and intimacy.

Characteristic designs of the glazed ceramics of the Middle Ages are evident: the islimi design, the rosettes with numerous leaves, but the basis of the ornamental cycle consists of new designs, essentially plant-like. In the modern ceramics of Richtan the tradition of making practical objects in the decorative manner has been maintained: vases and knives, for instance.

A detached painting displays these ornaments.

Snuffboxes. 1920s-30s. Samarkand.
Fine Arts Museum of the Uzbekistan
Republic. Tashkent.

The colours of the ceramics from the school of Bukhara and Samarkand differ fundamentally from the blue, white and azure ceramic of Ferghana and Kharezm, and may be recognized by a warm brown-yellowish range of colours, enhanced with painted patterns (Ghijduvan, Chakhri-Siabz, Urgut) or engraved designs (Denau, Kitab, Karatag).

The Uzbekan and Tadjikan modern potters vividly perceive the complex connection between ornamental design, colouring and form. In search of original solutions they look to the artistic heritage of far-off days. Moukhit Rachimov, an old master in perfect control of the ceramic technique, has crated original compositions based on a study of famous specimens of glazed ceramics form Aphrasiab and Merv. The work of this master, created in the ceramic styles of antiquity and the Middle Ages, is marked by its rich ornamentation and beauty of shape.

In this way the tradition of moulded "mountainous" ceramic, going back to the mists of time, has been preserved. Various forms of clay crockery - jugs, cups, bowls, stylized mourgobas - were made by hand; without using a potter's wheel, by the women of the mountainous regions of Tadjikistan.

This kind of pottery was often adorned with a brown-ochre coating and moulded applied details representing pearls, serpents and stylized figures of animals.

Nowadays metal traditional objects have lost their practical function and have become unique artworks, worthy of an exhibition, or souvenir articles.

Actually, aesthetic qualities of objects play an essential role: beauty of shape, refinement of ornamentation, traditional nature. The art of M. Atadjanov, one of the representatives of the old generation, is based on traditional chiselling techniques from Khiva: graceful forms, elegance and refinement of the engraved decoration. The works of M. Madaliev, a young carver from Kokand, reveal a radiant, optimistic vision of life and are an example on an original application of ancient traditions.

The goldsmith's trade is also flourishing. The goldsmith-jewellers work in the towns and regions of Uzbekistan and Tadjikistan, receiving orders for earrings, bracelets, rings, and other kings of jewellery. S. Sakhatov, A. Kourbankouliev, K. Ataev continue the traditions of the Turkman goldsmith's trade, enriching it with new techniques.

Their works are beautiful, refined and graceful and at the same time remain faithful to the style and character of popular art: simplicity, harmonious balance, brilliance and purity.

The manufacturing of carpets has enjoyed a real boom in the republics of Central Asia.

In 1920-1930 carpets were essentially made by guilds, but from the 1960s onwards, carpet manufacturers established themselves in Khiva, Chakhri-Siabz and other towns. The making of carpets continues at home on looms with handles. Nowadays the weavers perpetuate the ancient traditions and introduce new and original ideas. Industrial carpet-weaving firms have settled in the region of Kirghizstan, where carpet manufacturing used to be traditional. After the establishment of the Soviet regime, measures were taken in Turkmenistan to maintain and develop the important traditions of carpet manufacturing. In 1929 the carpet industry of the S.S.R. of Turkmenistan was established, including an artistic experimental workshop which later became the firm "Turkmen-kover". Looking for new solutions the craftsmen of 1930 - 1940 turned towards subject carpets. It is true that not all of them are successful, because of the eclecticism of style. The best efforts are those of D. Chakhberdyeva and B. Sabitova. The carpets are woven based on their designs with new patterns in the traditional framework. The same is valid for the manufacturing of hangings and printed cloth, with industrial production also based on tradition. In the villages, expert embroideresses perpetuate their knowledge of needlework. Golden embroidery as well lives through new organizational forms. Thus a factory in Bukhara produces essentially souvenir articles, decorative panels, curtains and national costumes for theatres and folk-groups. In Kirghizstan and Turkmenistan, the golden embroidery enriches the goods produced by industry: mural carpets, pillowcases, national head-dress, skirts and waistcoats, wallets - preserving the traditional procedures and decorative style.

Simultaneously, woodcarving has experienced a revival in Tadjikistan and Uzbekistan where the craft shows great originality, without betraying its traditional style. Many objects have a practical purpose, but most of them are intended for exhibitions or as souvenirs. This is also the case for traditional leather articles which are no longer used in everyday life. In the rural communities, the wooden objects of everyday usage, like chests, cupboards, crockery, cradles and toys, have radiant colours. The predominating colours which harmonize together are yellow, red and green. In the world of decoration we often encounter objects painted with patterns that were said to possess protective powers in the past. At rural fairs these days one can buy many articles which are nicely painted by popular craftsmen who perpetuate the skill of their ancestors. The development of popular decorative arts in the republics of Central Asia proves their vitality. Adopting new organizational procedures, they are integrated into everyday life and architecture. The popular arts thus become an inspirational source, sustaining the various disciplines of today's fine arts.

Musical instruments. 1960-70.
Museum of the Applied Arts of the
Uzbekistan Republic. Tashkent.

THREE PEARLS
ON THE SILK ROAD

SAMARKAND

The Blue City

With its 2,500 years of existence, Samarkand is one of the oldest cities of the world. It was invaded by the armies of Alexander the Great, sacked by the troops of the Arab Caliphate and by the Mongol hordes of Gengis Khan, but it was always reborn from its ashes to become, several times, the capital of the great States of Central Asia. And it remains, thanks to the invaluable wealth of its architecture and pictural patrimony, one of the greatest archaeological centres ever known.

In the beginning, Samarkand stretched along the valley of the Zeravshan River situated to the north of the actual town. Becoming more important, Samarkand spread increasingly until it occupied all the hill slopes, around the 9th century. The water supply of the Zeravshan River had necessitated the building of a viaduct and its destruction by the Mongols meant, for a while, the death of the city. About a hundred years later, the consequences of this invasion were obliterated.

Samarkand rose on its old site, not far from the (supposed) sacred sepulchre of Kussam-Ibn-Abbas. The building of the necropolis of Shah-e-Zendeh was undertaken - the more important period being situated in the last part of the 14th century - with the mausoleums built for the Timurid military chiefs and great noblemen of the time constituting one of the major contributions to its architectural richness; several parts of this ensemble date from Ulug-Beg (first half of the 15th century). They include in particular a decorated portal at the foot of a hill and a mausoleum with two turquoise cupolas that are supposed to be the tombs of the astronomer Kazy-zade-Roumi, master of Ulug-Beg. But the best preserved mausoleum is without question the one of Shadi-Mulk-Aka dating from 1372 and his mother Turkan-Aka, Timur's sister. The portal surface is of baked clay glazed and chiselled. The inside is decorated with majolica.

The passage between the mausoleums opens on a little shaded yard, shut by the Tuman-Aka mausoleum dating from the beginning of the 14th century and by mausoleums of the pre-Timurian epoch, among which is the Khodja-Ahmad.

A sculpted door built in 1404-1405, initially encrusted with ivory, leads to a 15th century mosque and to the Mausoleum of Kussam-ibn-Abbas which is the principal and most ancient of Samarkand. Unique, the polychrome glaze coating of Shah-e-Zendeh evokes its creators' talents.

Detail of the façade of the Shah-e mausoleum in Zinda, Samarkand.

Pages 196, 197:
Views from the most majestic place in
central Asia: 'The Registan'.

Following pages:
Right of the square, the Shir Dor madrasah. 17th century.

Previous pages:
Left of the square, the Ulug-Beg
madrasah. 15th century.

Gur i-Emir mausoleum and Tamerlan
tomb.

It also testifies to the artistic mastery of this generation of builders who succeeded one another during this period and knew how to unite the edifices in a great architectural ensemble without any false note. In the 14th century Samarkand became the capital of the Timur Empire. In five years of a colossal work (1399-1404) the congregational mosque of Bibi-Khanum (Timur's [Tamerlan's] Chinese wife) and the mausoleum of Timur himself, known as the Gur i-Emir, were built. This mausoleum was to become the sepulchre of his sons, his grandson and himself. A fine example of the town-planning culture of Central Asia is Registan Square with its groups of monumental buildings: the madrasahs (Muslim schools) of Ulug-Beg (1417-20), Shir Dor (1619-to 1636) and Tilla Kari (17th century) which border the square on three sides. During the 15th century, under Ulug-Beg, less important buildings were erected but they distinguish themselves by their noble proportions and the harmony of their glazed polychrome coatings. Splendid too are the portals, the vast, coloured domes and the remarkable exterior decoration in majolica, mosaic, marble and gold.

An observatory - a rare construction - was to have been erected by Ulug-Beg near Samarkand but that project was abandoned after his assassination and the remains of the building didn't resist time; its vestiges disappeared during the 15th century.

Parallel to the monumental constructions of the 15th century, small edifices were erected throughout the town, with clear and picturesque settings that still bear the marks of a subtle artistic sense. The ensemble of Khodja-Abd-e-Darun is one example. In the 16th century, Bukhara being the capital of the dynasty, Samarkand suffers from the new political change and many edifices are abandoned.

On the Registan was erected the Shir Dor madrasah in place of the Khanaka of Ulug-Beg. The edifice, which is situated opposite the madrasah of Ulug-Beg, displays great continuity in its facade, proportions and style. The third side of the square is occupied by the Tilla Kari madrasah named for the lavish gilding that adorned the rest of the edifice.

Since the 18th century, Samarkand has been settled in its glorious past. The monumental architecture of the capital of Uzbekistan was never again enriched by monuments equal to those which made its greatness and which gave it the prestigious name of the Blue City because of the ceramic tiles of its copulas reflecting the sky.

Previous pages:
Ceiling of Gur I-Emir, detail.
Timur mausoleum.

Gur Emir mausoleum.

Following page:
Registan Square. In the middle of the square, Tilla Kari madrasah. 17th century.

BUKHARA

The Citadel of the Arch

Bukhara was founded in the beginning of the Christian era, and was, throughout the 6th century, the capital of a powerful kingdom. The town is constructed around an old citadel which still towers above the rest of the city. Very quickly, thanks to its flourishing commerce, Bukhara stretched out beyond its surrounding walls to constitute, from the 7th century onwards, several active inner suburbs (*rabades*) where the local craft industry could develop comfortably. But caution required that this new town should be protected in its turn. Therefore, new ramparts, which have been partly preserved, were constructed in the 8th century. Pre-Mongolian architecture remains, and amongst the buildings of the 9th and 10th century one can still admire the mausoleum of the Samanides. It has great artistic value and is harmoniously constructed with terracotta bricks. Thanks to its proportions and conception it constitutes one of the masterpieces of Central Asian architecture.

In 1127, the construction of the Kalian minaret represented a testimonial of its time. Its powerful trunk nine meters in diameter at its base, becomes narrower as it thrusts up to attain a high of 46 meters. Admirable because of its original brickwork, it has stood the test of time, due to the consummate artistry of its builders, without undergoing any restoration.

Beyond the walls of the city, there is a mosque (*namazga*) constructed in 1119-1120, embellished in the 16th century with a gallery consisting of a triple tier of arches. The portal on the south side of the mosque Magoki-Attari is characteristic of 12th century architecture with its many decorations. Its adornments are remarkable for a delicacy of decorative techniques. The rare preserved monuments of this era in Bukhara bear witness to great architectural mastery and a subtle art of decoration.

Aerial view of Bukhara.

Following pages:
Bukhara, view towards iwân, giving access to the the madrasah of the great mosque.

The Arch of the Citadel.

Previous page:
Abdulla-Khan madrasah. 17th century.

Page 220: Details period

Bukhara, ceiling.

The post-Mongolian era in Bukhara and other towns of Central Asia was not a period of important constructions. One had to wait until the 15th century for the cultural genius to resume so that particularly the monumental arts could develop rapidly. Under the reign of Ulug-Beg the town obtains a new Muslim college (madrasah), with design and decoration specific to the revival of the epoch.

In the 16th century, after the accession of the Uzbek Cheibanides dynasty, Bukhara again became the capital of the vast state of Central Asia. The town grew and new ramparts were erected. The mosque built in 1514 next to the Kalian minaret became the most important one of the whole region. In 1535-1536, on the other side of the square, the Muslim college Miri-Arab was built. Today it still emanates, together with the mosque and the minaret facing it, incomparable grandeur. Other Muslim colleges were also built according to the gemel construction principle (also called the koch technique): the Modari-Zaineddin madrasah in 1566-1567, and the Abdulla-Khan madrasah in 1588-1590.

The architecture of small urban mosques combined monumental construction techniques with popular traditions, as was the case with the mosques of Baliand and Khodja-Zaïneddin. Their interior ornamentation is equal to the decorations of the best constructions of Samarkand in the 15th century.

In the 16th century, takis were quite important: civil buildings like caravanserais and public baths. Without claiming to adhere to a specific artistic influence, their volume and decoration are expressive.

The buildings of Liabi-khaouz, which represent one of the biggest construction areas of town, date from the 17th century. The oldest - and the most extensive one of the whole of Central Asia - is the Muslim college Kukeldash (1568-1569). A lake, paved with chalky stones and bordered with trees was part of its property in 1620, while the Khanaka mosque and the Muslim college Nadir-divan-bech completed the harmony of the place shortly thereafter.

The four onion-domed towers overlooking the central dome (19th century) of Tchor-Minor. Entrance to the Calife-Niazkul madrasan.

Detail of lantern dome in Tchachma-Ayoub mausoleum.

Following pages:
Poi-Kalian complex.
12th – 20th century.

Kalian mosque. 16th century.

Detail of faience portal of the Divan Begi madrasah.

Divan Begi madrasah.

Page 228: Abdulla-Khan madrasah. 16th century.

Page 230: Samanides mausoleum. Early Middle Ages motif.

Page 232: Tchar-Bakr. 16th century.

In 1652, the Muslim college Abdulazis-khan was erected on this quadrilateral, facing Ulug-Beg. The unity created by these buildings of rigorous architecture and traditional inspiration remains unrivalled in the 18th century.

All these buildings give Bukhara its amplitude and style. Their layout provides an impression of grandeur hardly ever equalled anywhere. Besides, the carefully considered placement of these buildings conditions the town planning and structures the main roads and squares of the town around them. Restored today, these civil and religious buildings represent Bukhara's cultural heart.

KHIVA

Cultural Capital of Kharezm

According to archaeological data, the city existed in the 6th-8th century, but it was not before the 17th century that it became the capital of the khanate of Khiva and it was not an important cultural centre before the 19th century. However its architectural vestiges are very surprising by their monumental character. They still occupy the oldest part of the town near the eastern gates of Palvan-Darvaza and along the street leading to the western gates.

No other town in Central Asia offers areas better preserved than Itchan-Kala of Khiva; this historical architecture of the old feudal towns is an invaluable testimony to its founding epoch. The only remains of that period are the mausoleum of Cheik Seid Allahuddin (14th century) famous for its sepulchre in majolica and the Crypt of the Governors where the funeral monuments of the ancients Khans were transferred.

Kalta-Minar minaret.

Islam-Khodja minaret.

A caravanserai protruding from the mass of the Itchan-Kala's walls was built near the Palvan-Darvaza gates. A covered passage called *tim* ended the central facade. The eye is enticed by the harmonious portal of the madrasah of Alla-Kuli-Khan. The palace of Alla-Kuli-Khan, Tash-Kauli, was erected in 1830-1840. This edifice offers living quarters as well as official rooms united by several little courtyards. There are also a harem, the *mikhmankhana*, for the Khan's reception, the *arrzhana* for legal proceedings, annexes and numerous passages to connect the diverse parts of the building.

This vast construction also contains the gallery Palvan-Darvaza, the Alla-Kuli-Khan madrasah and the Kutlug-Murad-Inak madrasah.

Near the western gates, destroyed today, remains the Kunia-Ark, encircled by a crenellated wall. This old fortress, which was a part of the Akchikh-Baba castle, was the ancient centre of the town.

Minaret of the Islam-Khodja madrasah.

View of Muhammed Rahim Khan II's madrasah.

Following page:
View of the city of Khiva.

237

In 1825 the inner part of Pakhlavan-Makhmud mausoleum was entirely decorated with majolica flagstones ornamented with typical Kivian motives. The edifices' cupolas were covered with turquoise tiles and the portal was enhanced with majolica.

Other notable buildings are still standing around the public square along the main avenue of Itchan-Kala, such as the Djuma mosque and its minaret, erected in the 18th century. The ceiling of the mosque, built in brick without any ornaments, is sustained by two hundred and twelve wood columns - about twenty of them are still there with their original carving. In the south and east of Kunia-ark, stand the Amin-Khan madrasah built in 1851-52 and the Seid Mohammed-Rakhim-Khan II madrasah erected twenty years later.

Monuments were continually erected in Khiva, testimony to its artistic genius. Between 1804 and 1812 the Hodjambedybi madrasah and the Kutlug-Murad-Inak madrasah were built. In 1806 the addition of a long gallery to the Palvan-Darvaza gates was realised, sheltering the commercial places under its numerous cupolas. In the middle of the 19th century, that was the beating heart of the city.

Islam-Hodja erected the highest minaret in Khiva. Fifty meters tall, it entirely dominated Itchan-Kala, its numerous monumental buildings and its isolated edifices. Today this architectural unity gives it an archaeological status practically unique in the art of Central Asia.

Other parts of Khiva, such as Dickam-Kala, are embellished by pools and greenery. Private constructions, reinforced by a long tradition, retain their characteristics: columns, struts, doors and other pieces of wood are often decorated with magnificent sculpture. Anxious to develop the ability of their ancestors, craftsmen and artists of Khiva carry on to make it useful and to perpetuate it.

Entrance into the heart of the
Phalavan Mahmoud mausoleum.

Following page:
General view of Khiva, cultural capital
of the Kharezm.

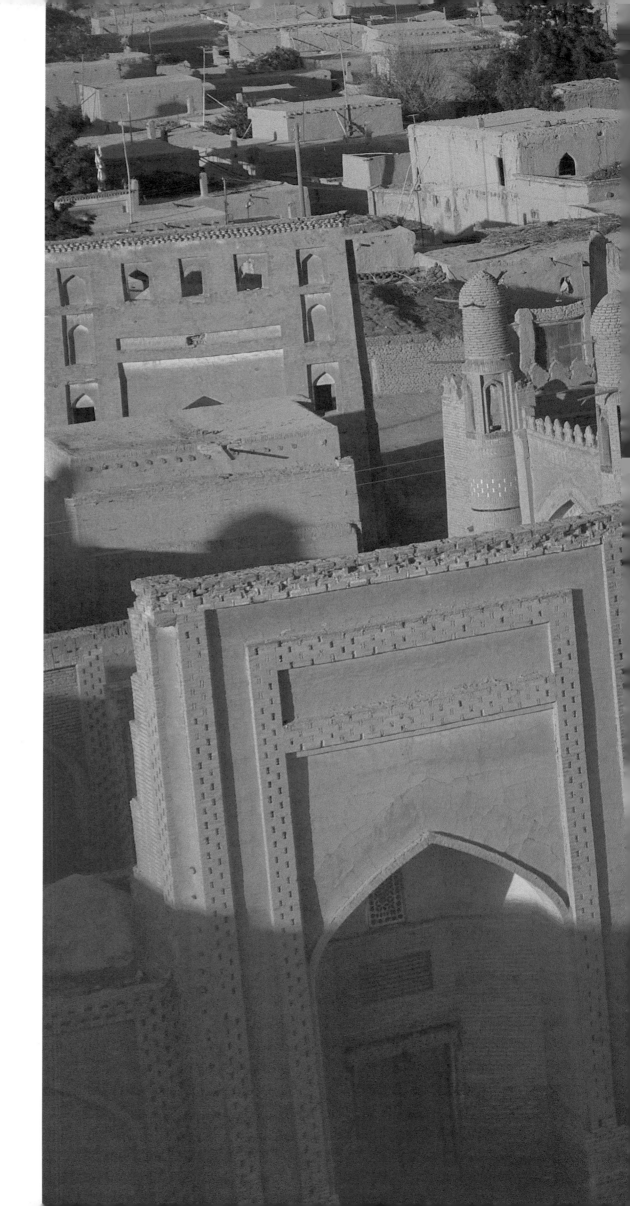

The Palace of Tâsh Khâvli, harem class.

INDEX

Door way of Tach-Darvis.

Following page:
The old Khiva city walls.

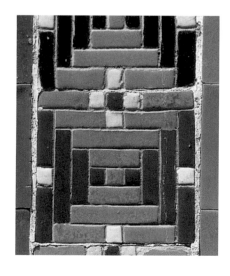

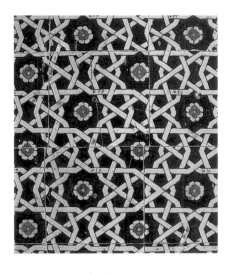

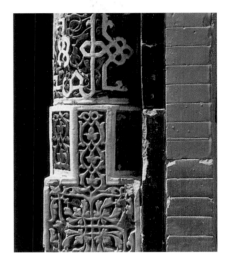

FEDERAL REPUBLIC OF RUSSIA

KAZAKHSTAN

• Akrau

AZERBAIJAN

• Turkestan

UZBEKISTAN

• Khiva

Tashkent

TURKMENISTAN

Samarkand

Bukhara

TADZ

• Ashkhabad

Dusanbe

IRAN

AFGHANISTAN

254

MONGOLIA

AUTONOMOUS CHINESE
PROVINCE OF XINJIANG

• Almaty

• Bishkek

KIRGIZIA

ISTAN

PAKISTAN   TIBET

INDIA